Have a question or concern? Let us know.
FritzenPublishing.com | support@fritzenpublishing.com

Hi Everyone,

Thank you so much for purchasing this Jade Summer book!

We have a surprise for you...

This book includes a **free digital copy** (PDF format) so you can print your favorite images and color them an unlimited number of times.

Make sure to visit our website to preview our other books, view completed coloring pages from fans, and follow the Jade Summer brand on social media.

JadeSummer.com

Yours Truly,

The Team at Jade Summer

P.S. Do you know someone who would enjoy this book? Buy them a copy and make it a surprise gift. We promise they'll love it!

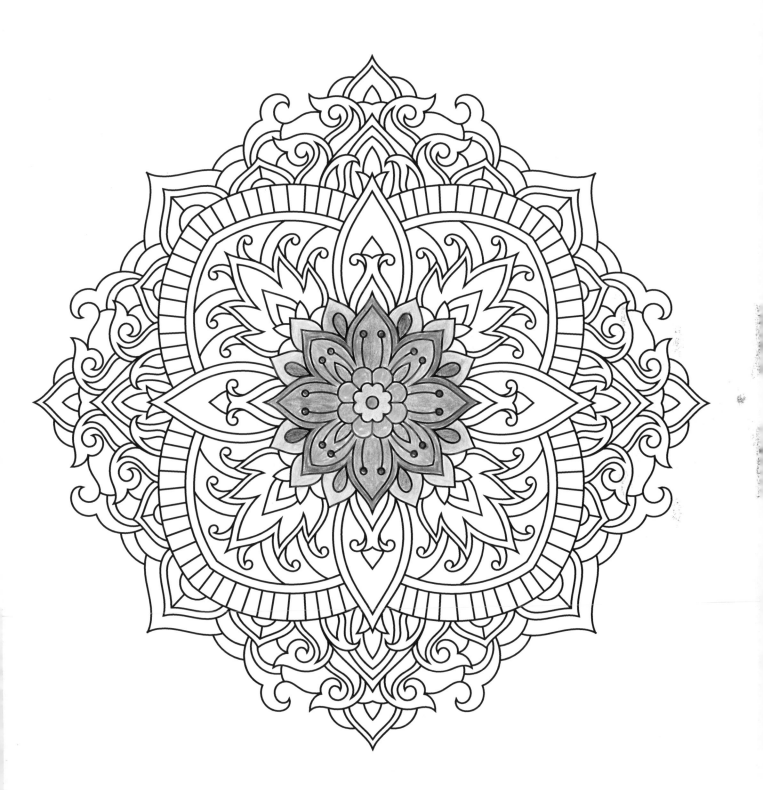

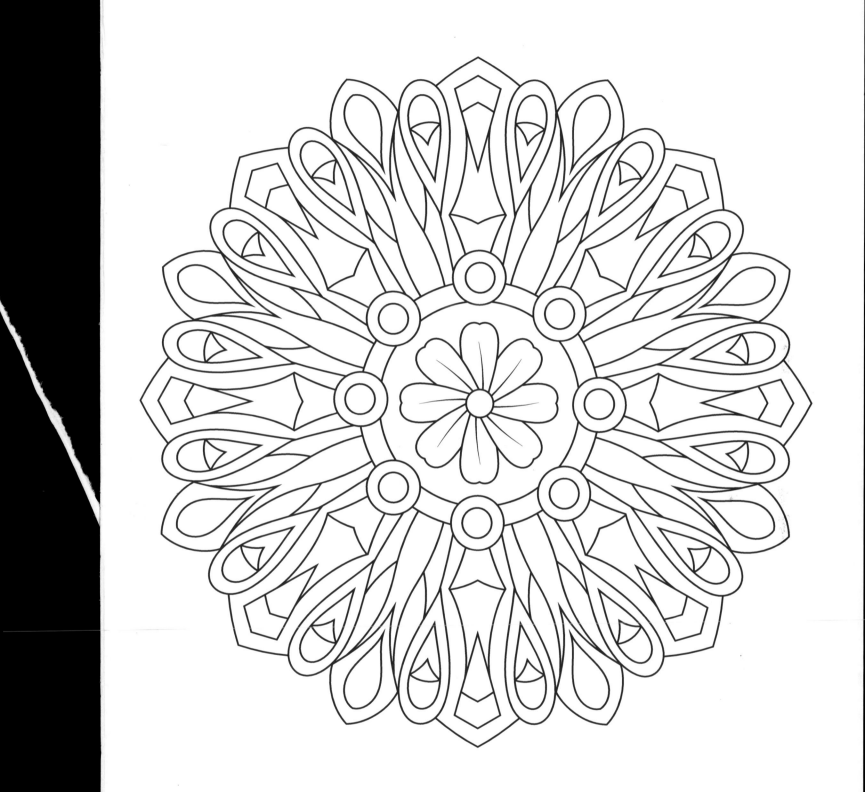

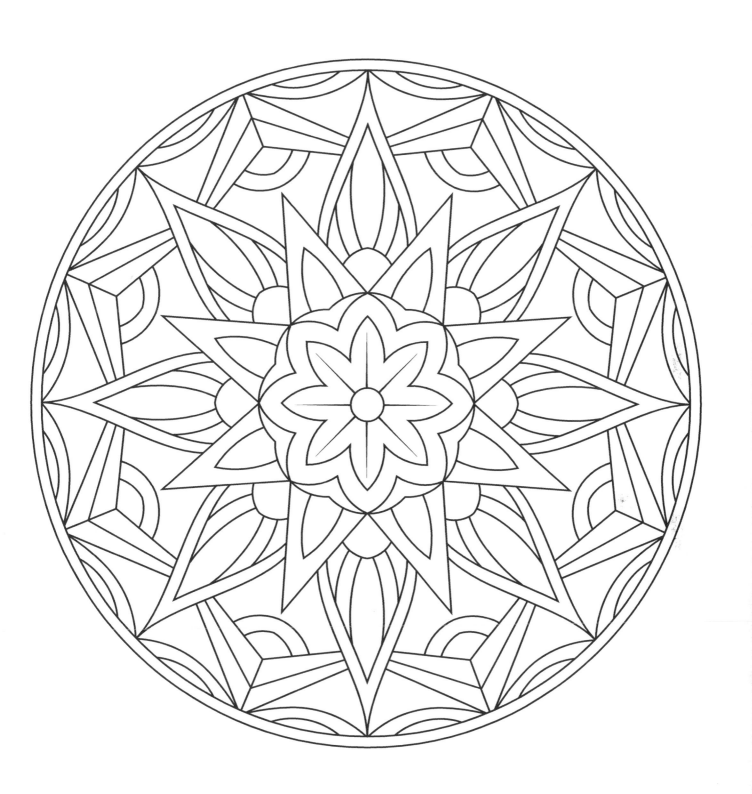

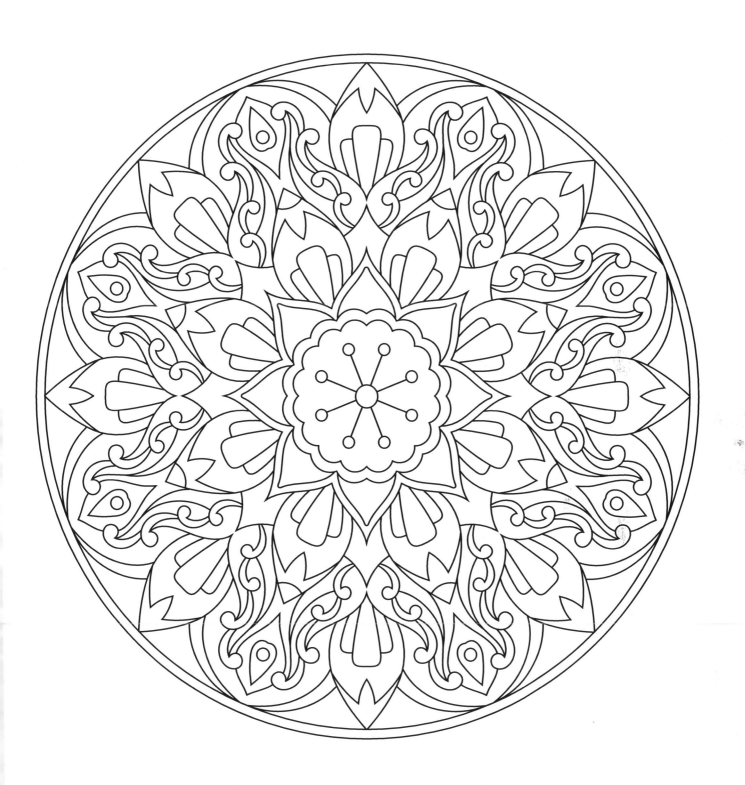

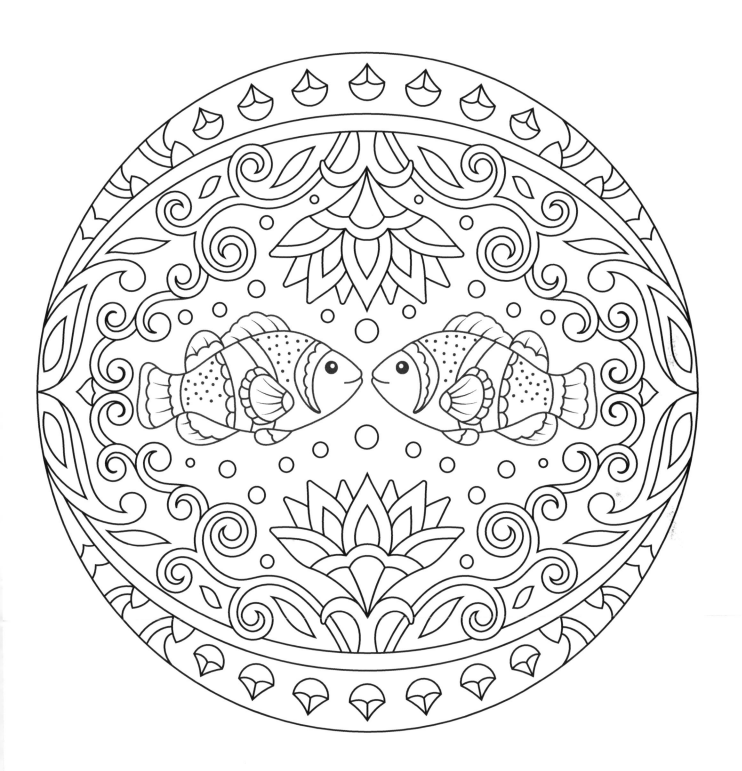

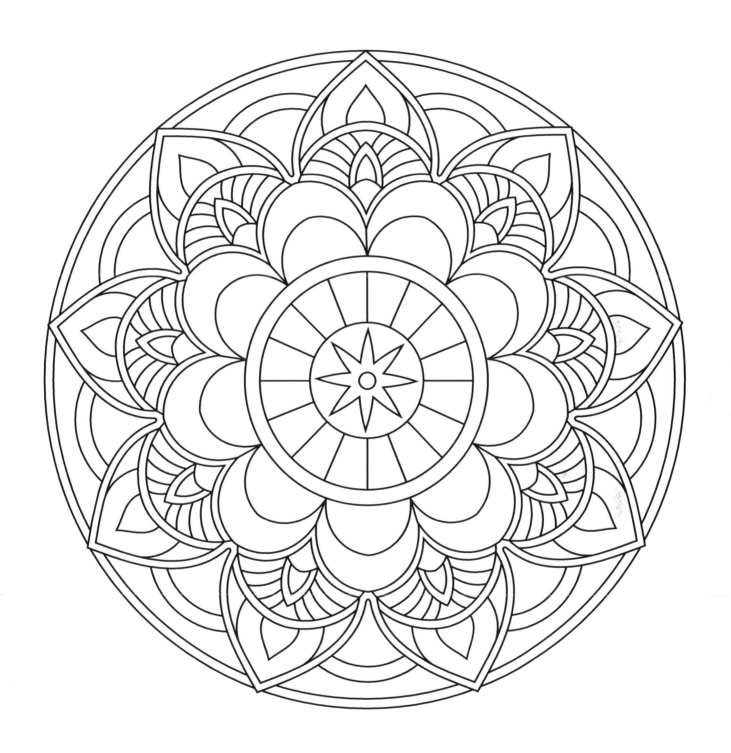

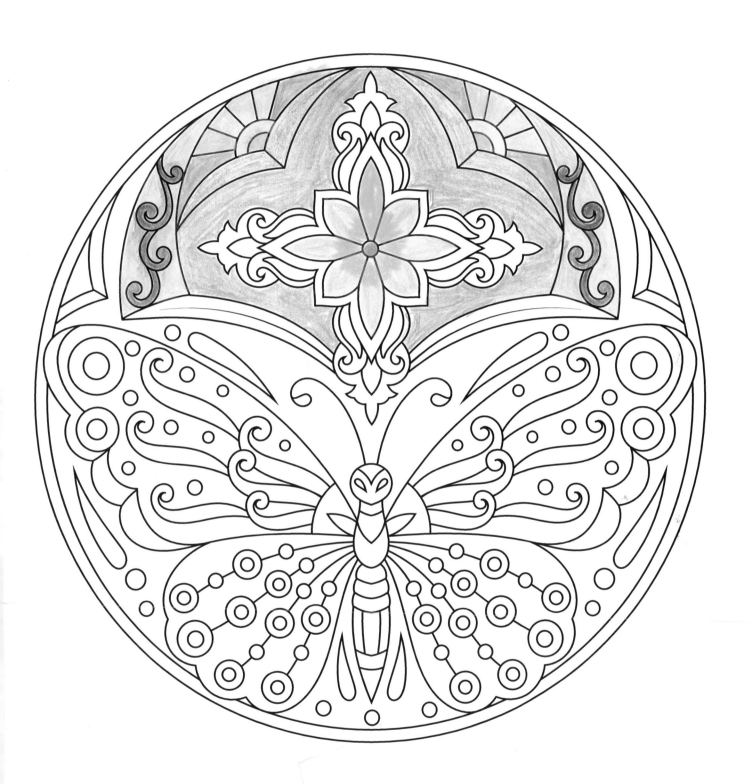

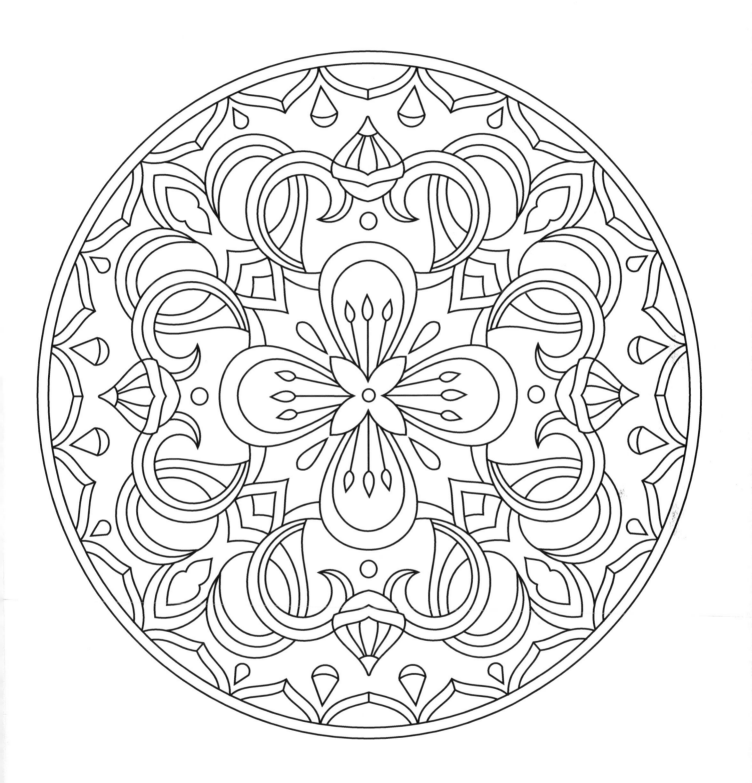

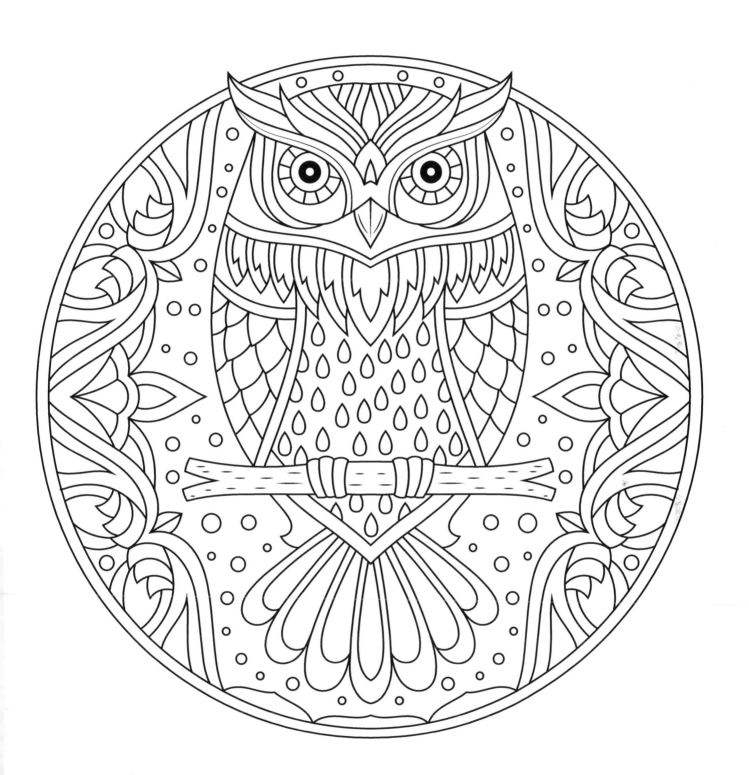

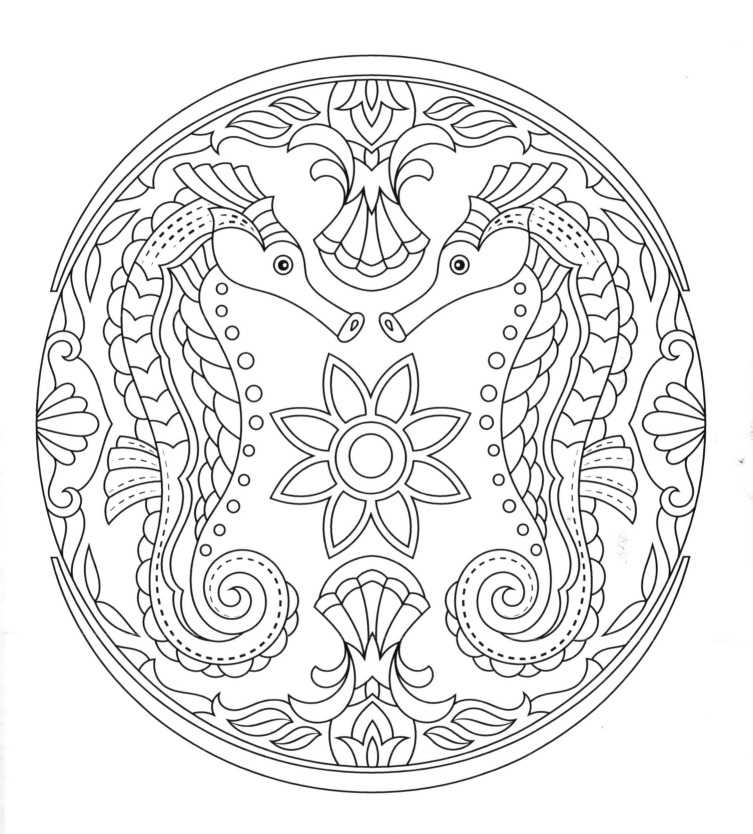

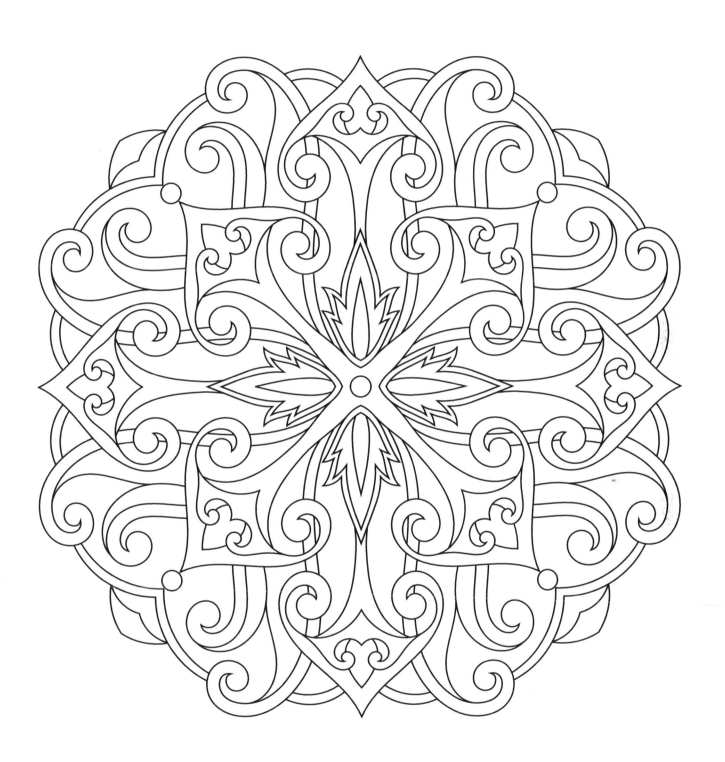

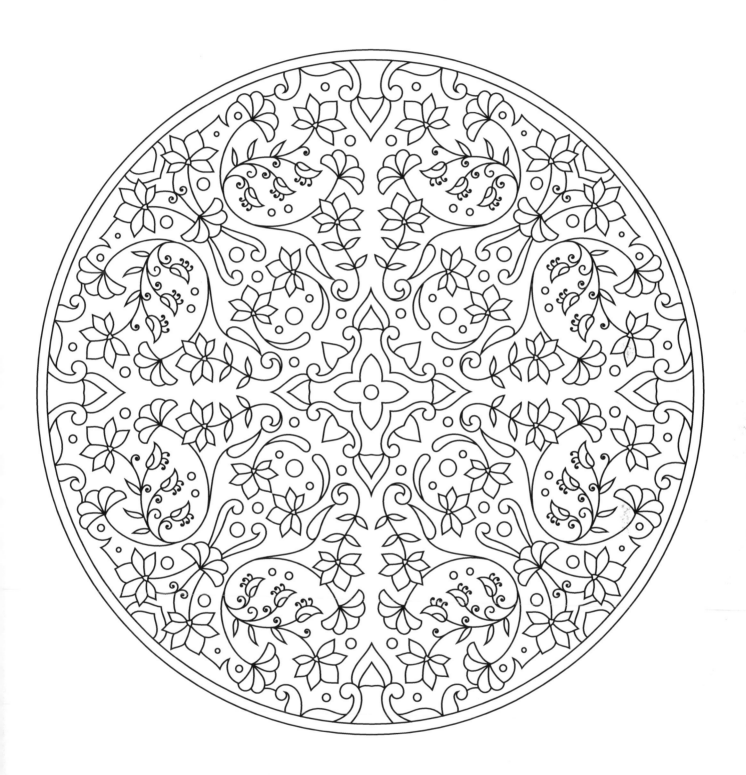

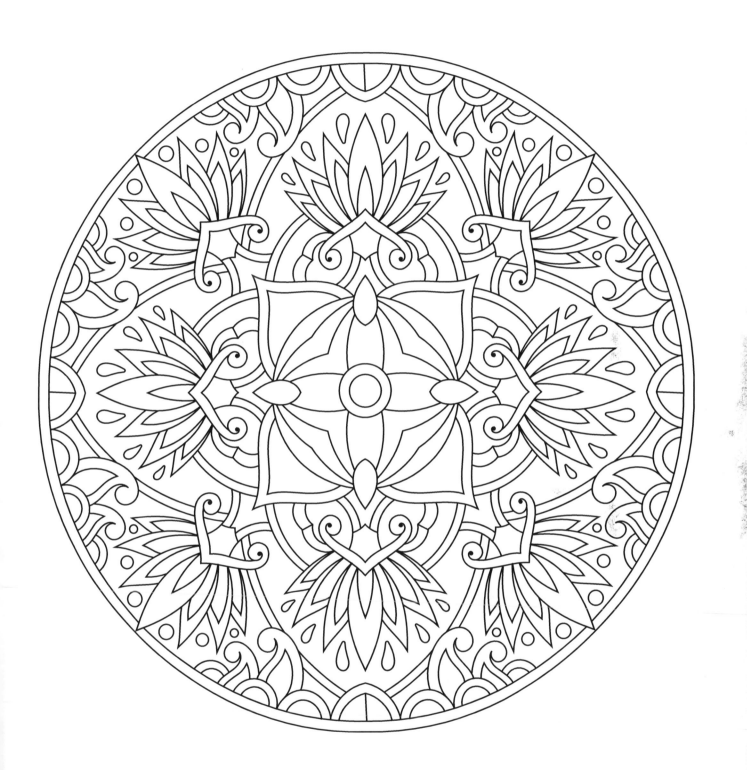

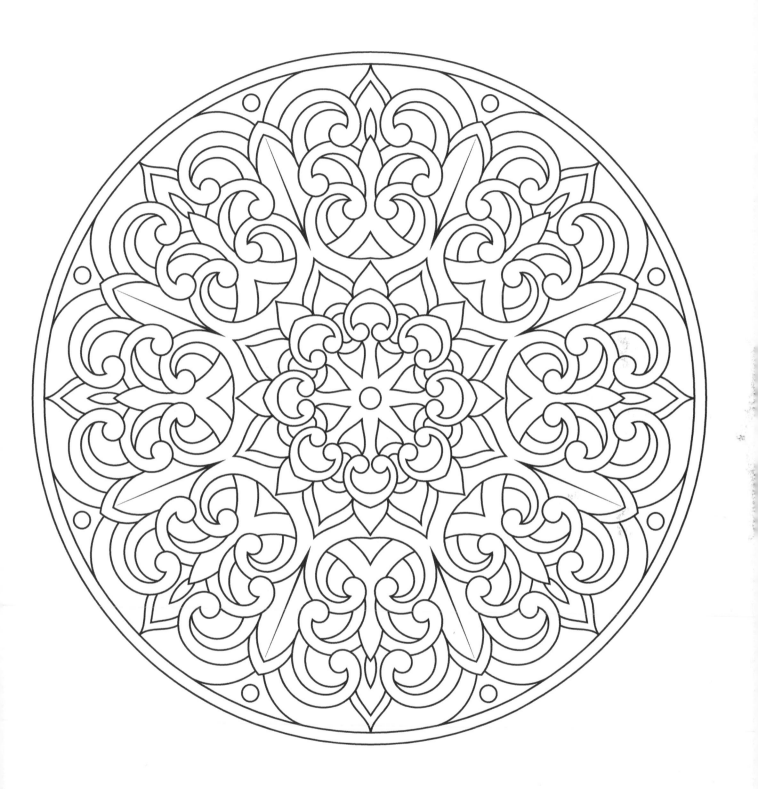

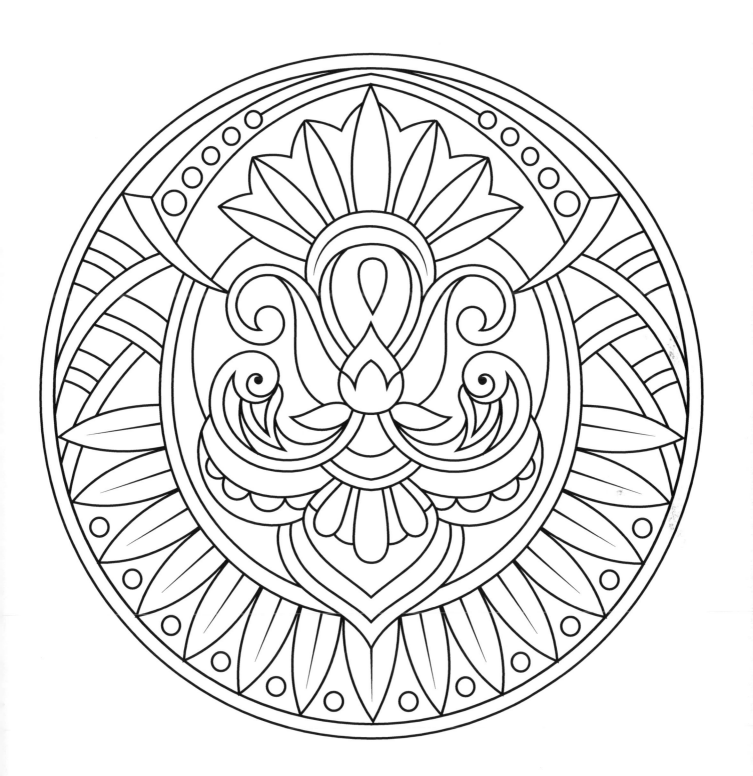

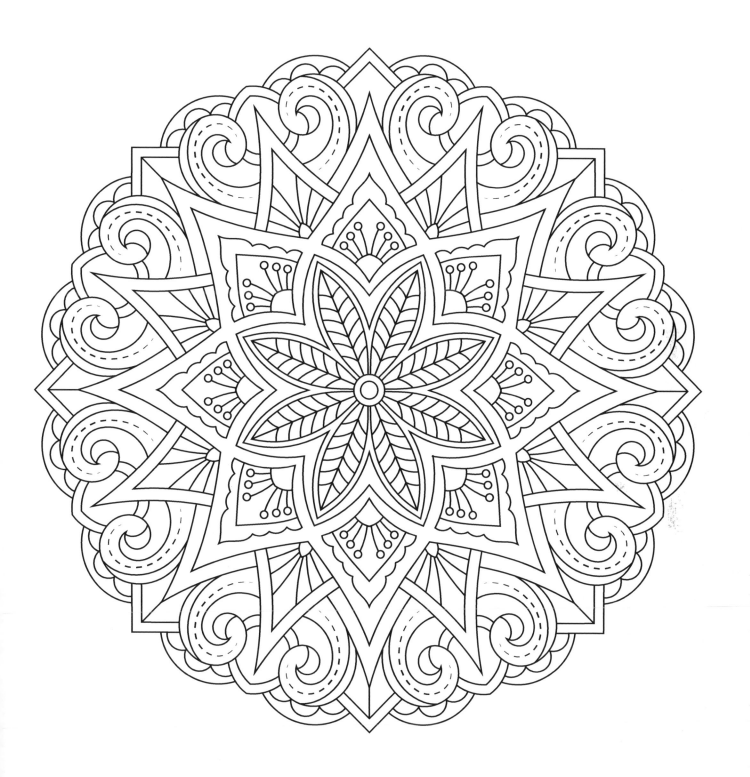

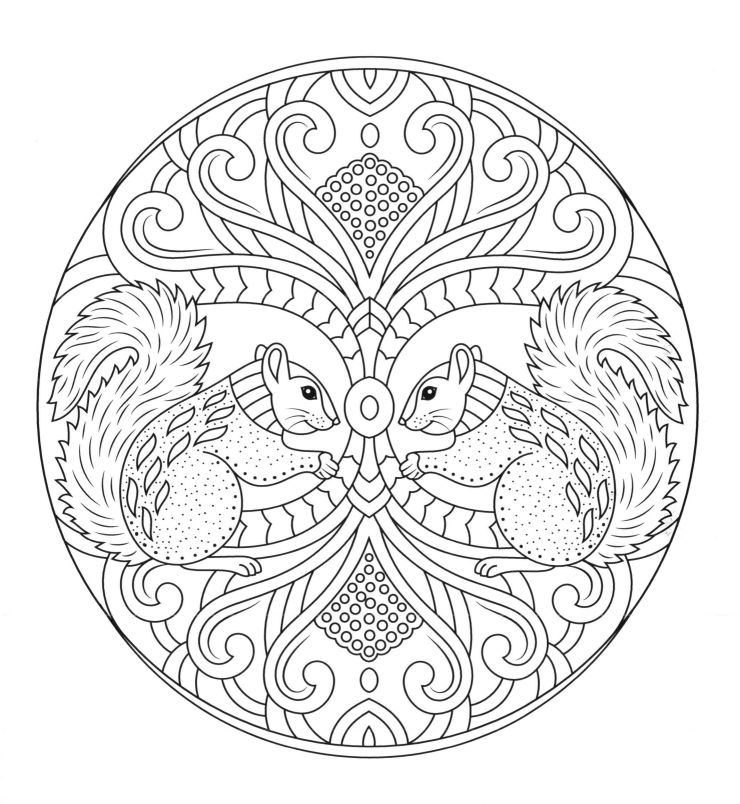

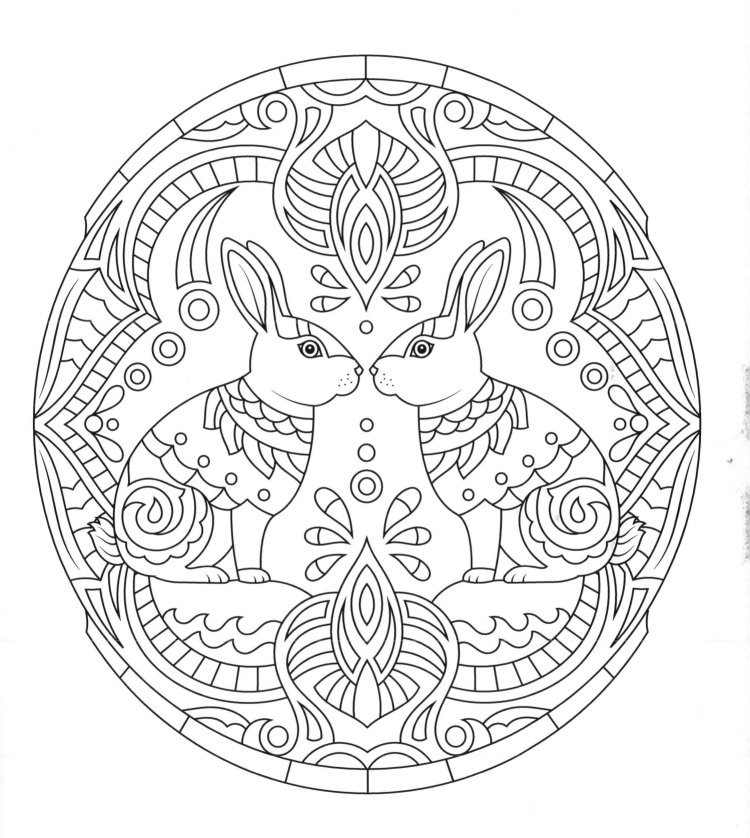

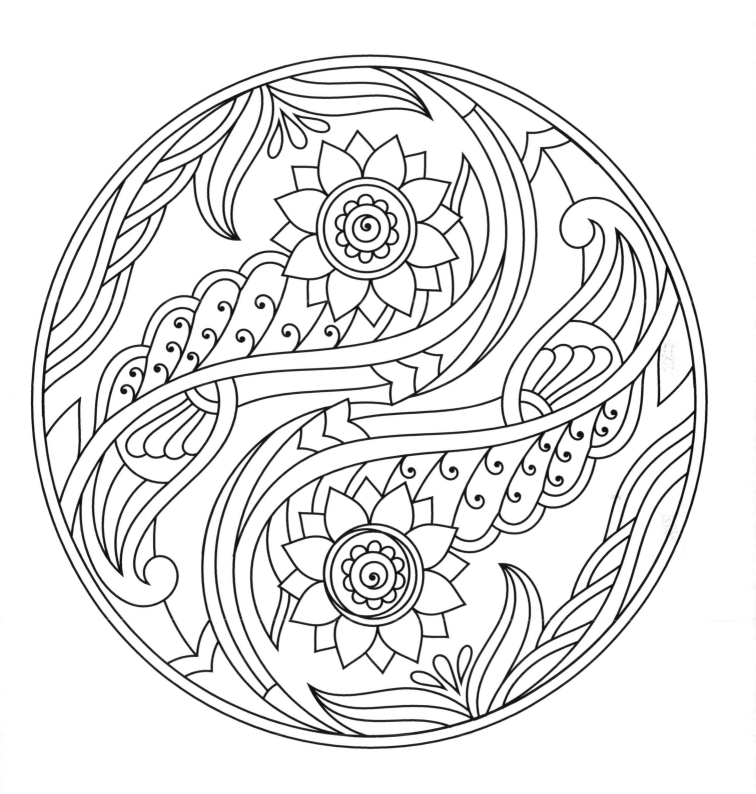

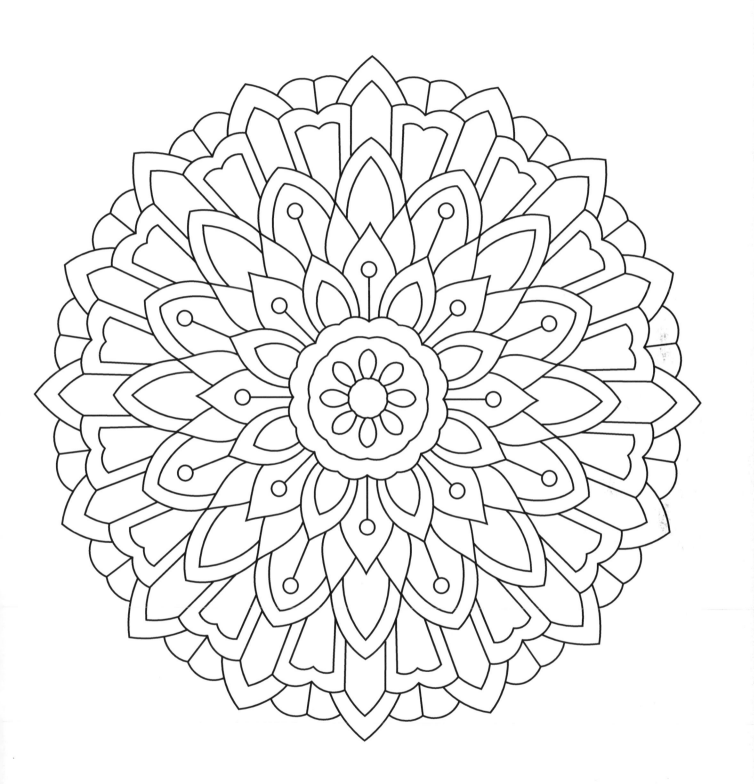

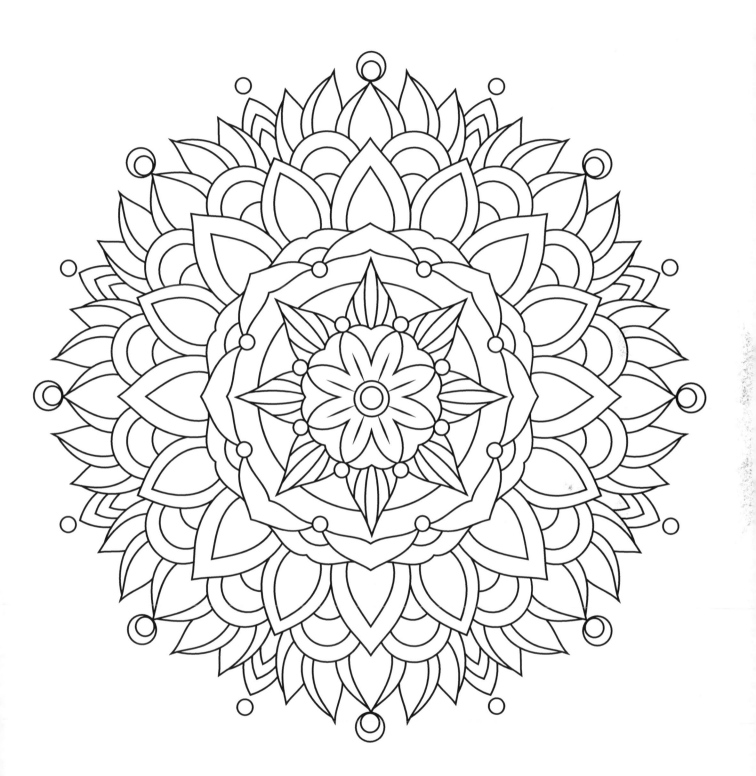

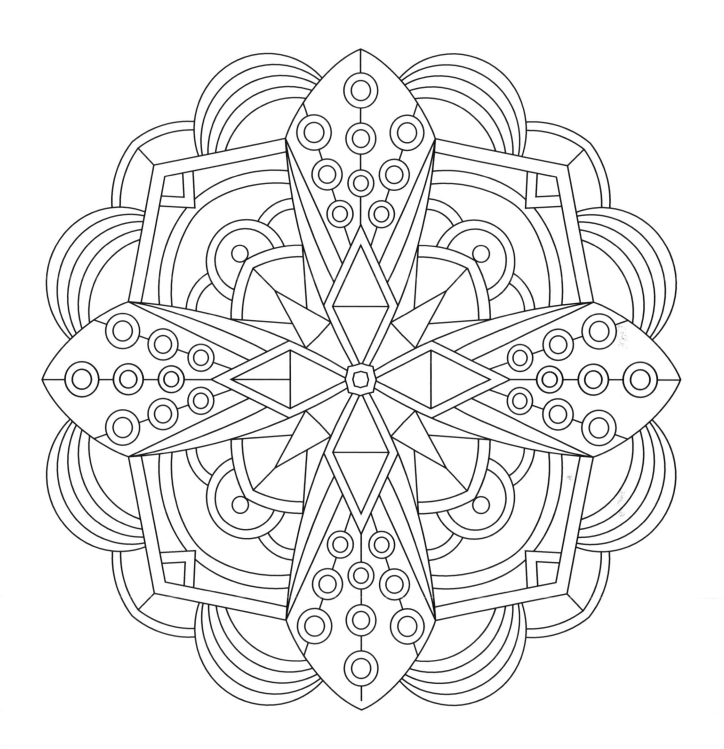

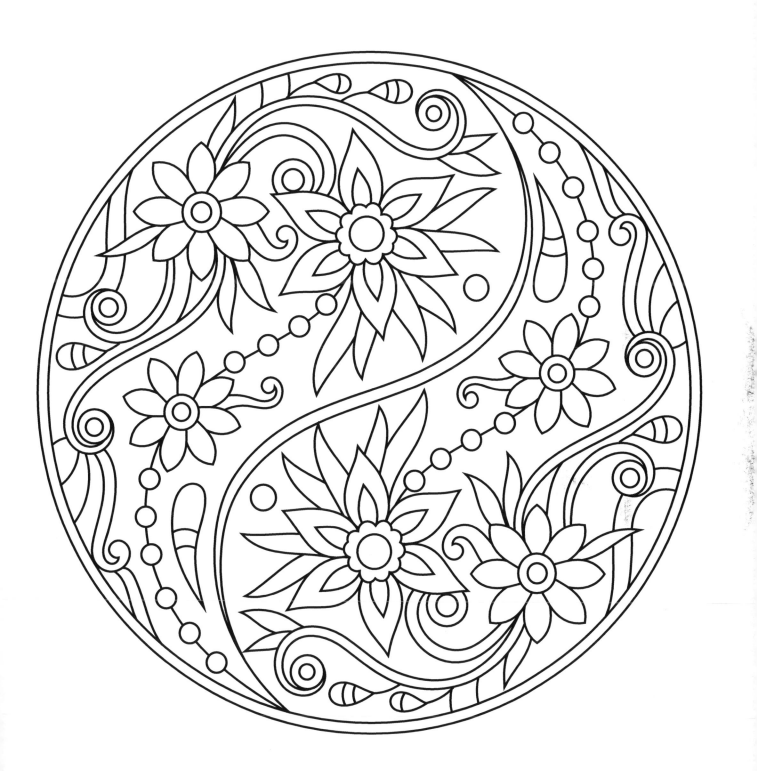

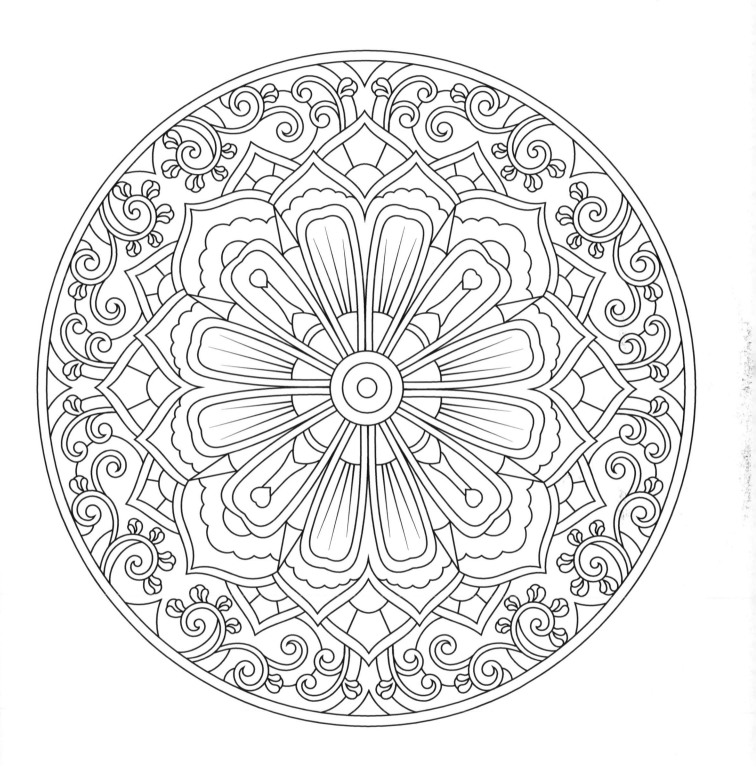

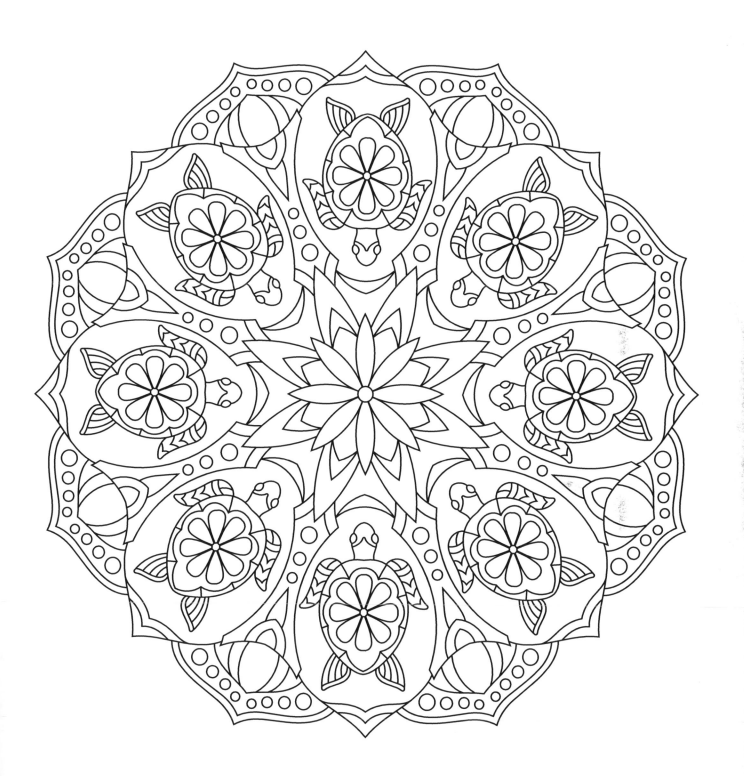

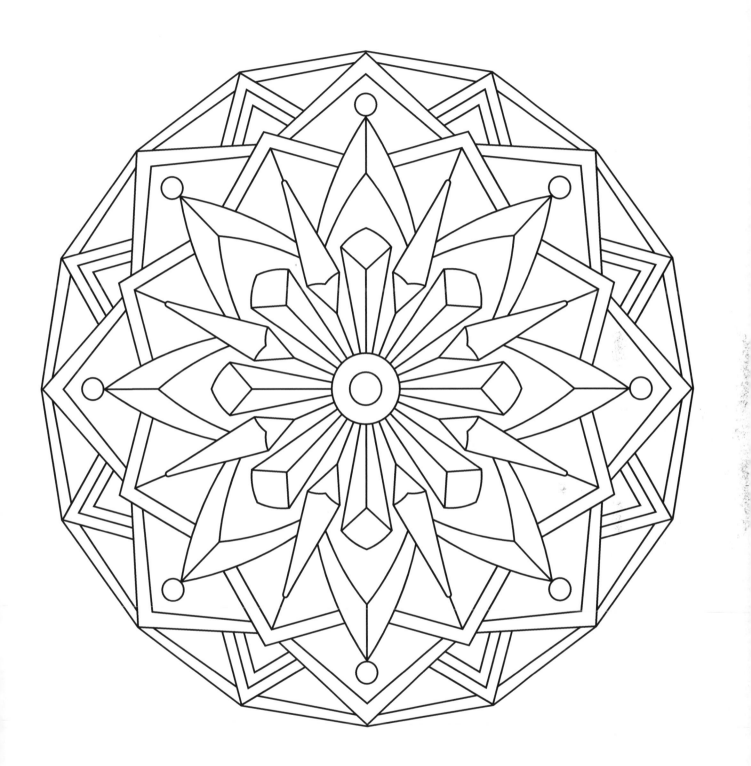

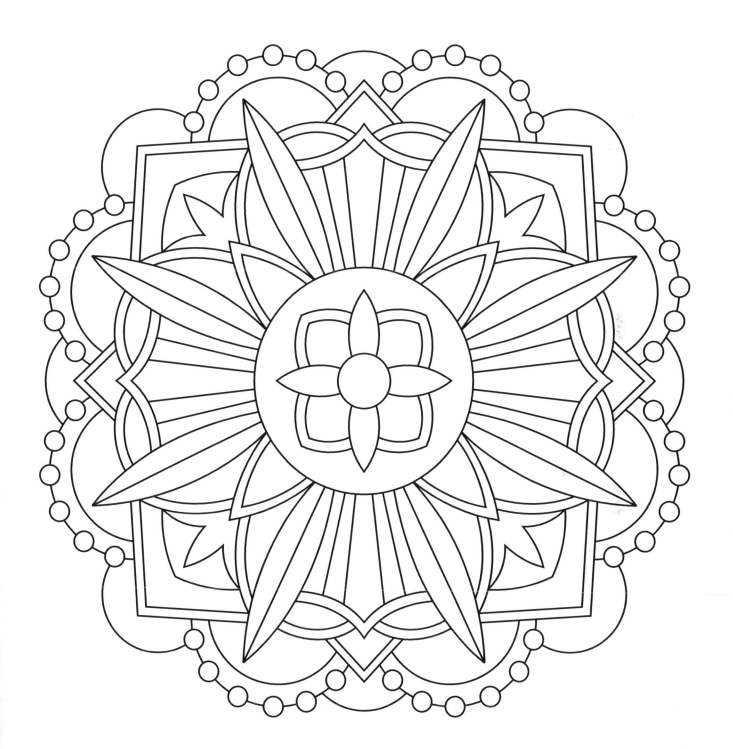

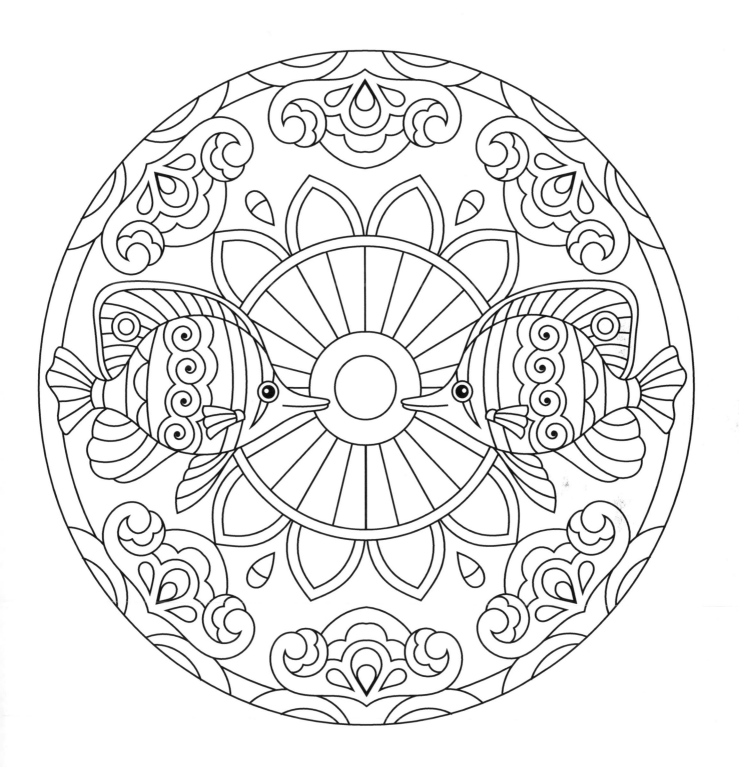

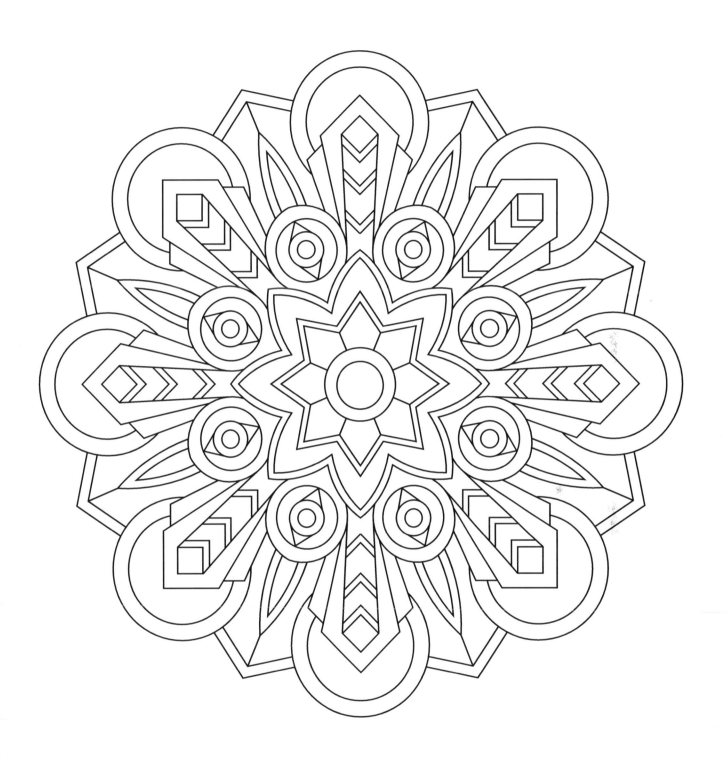

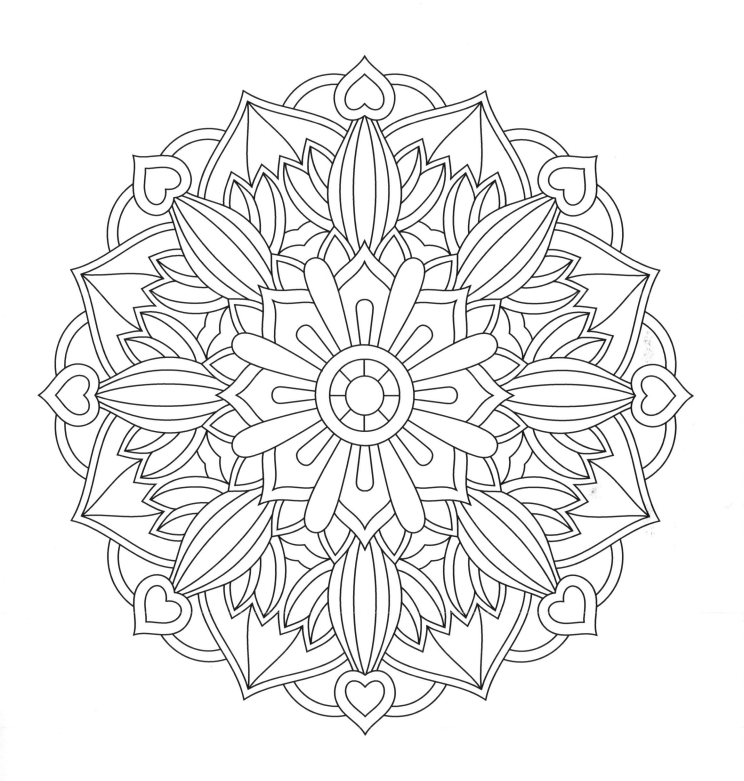

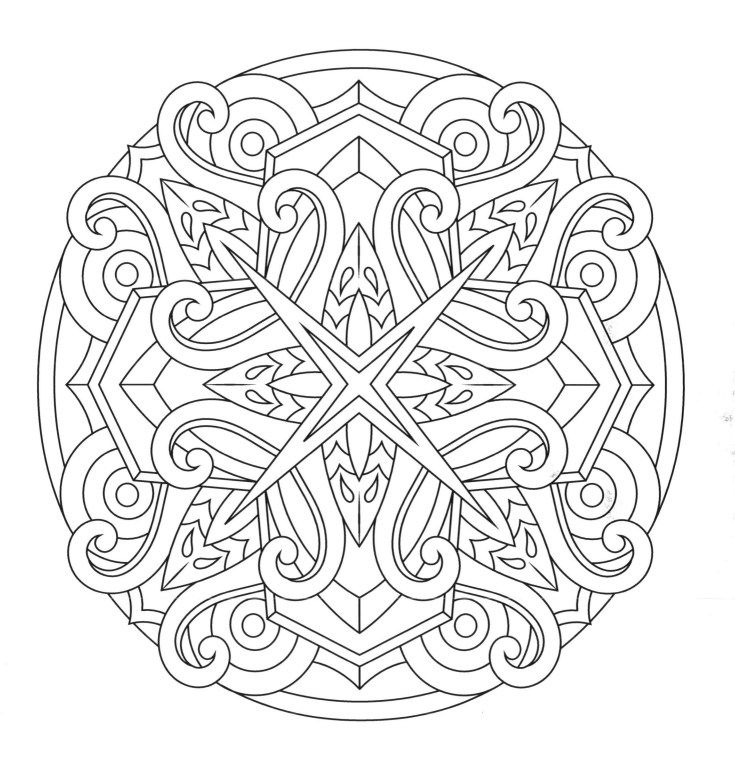

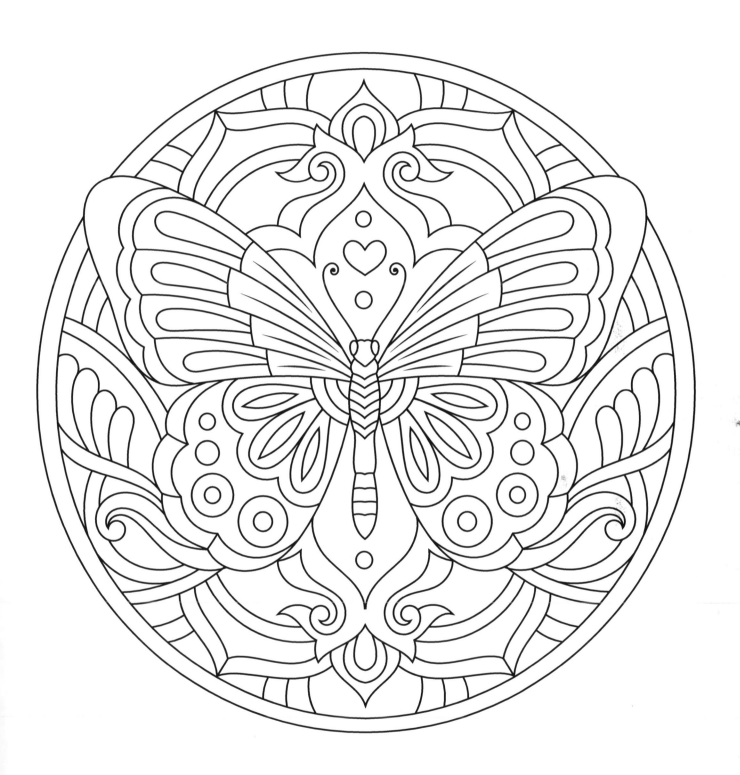

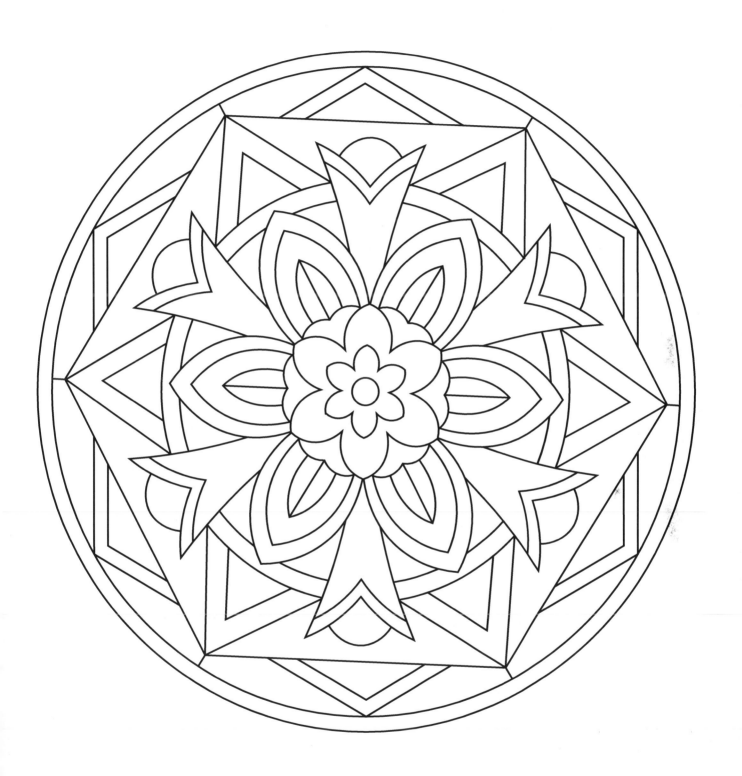

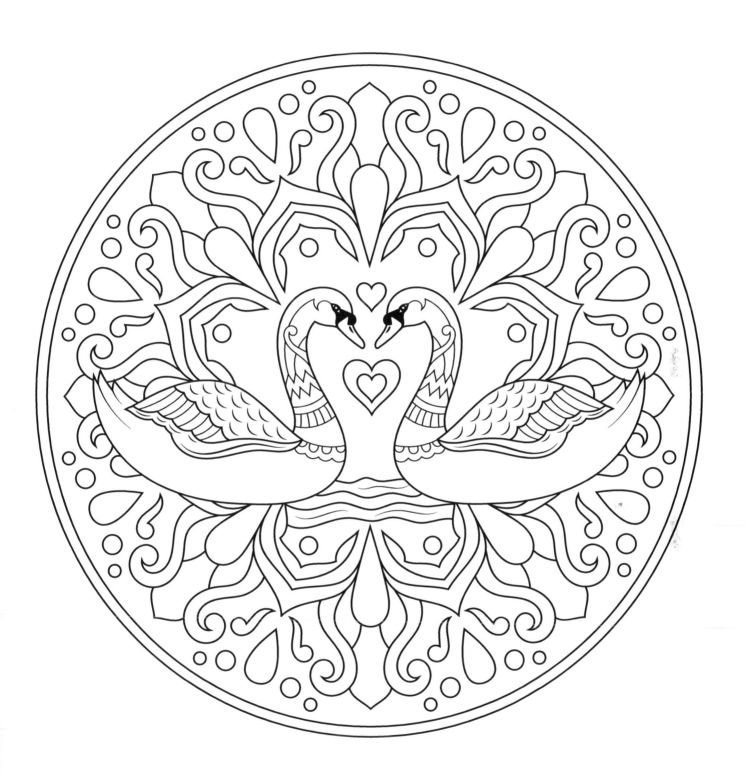

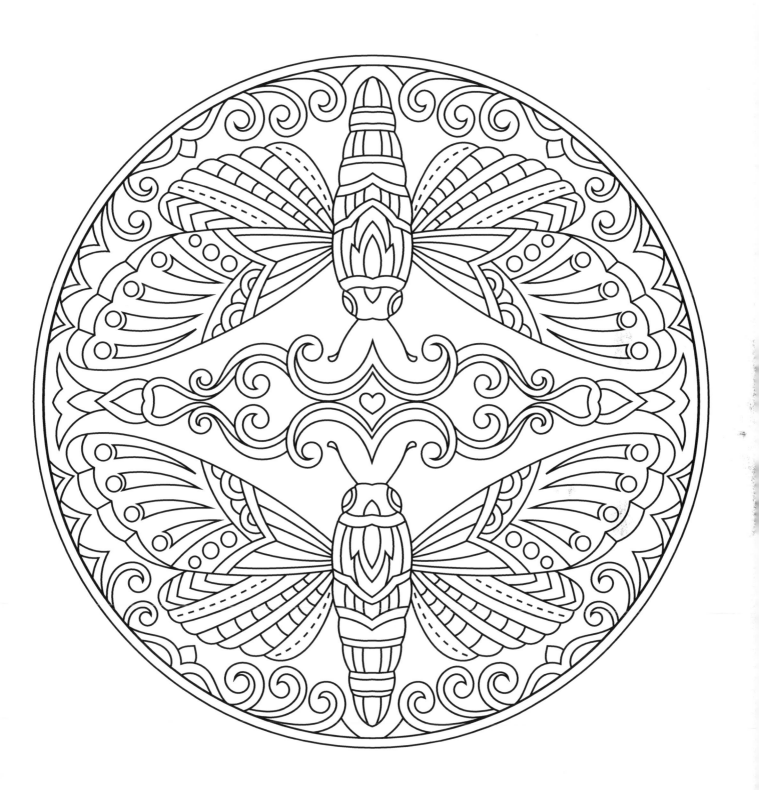

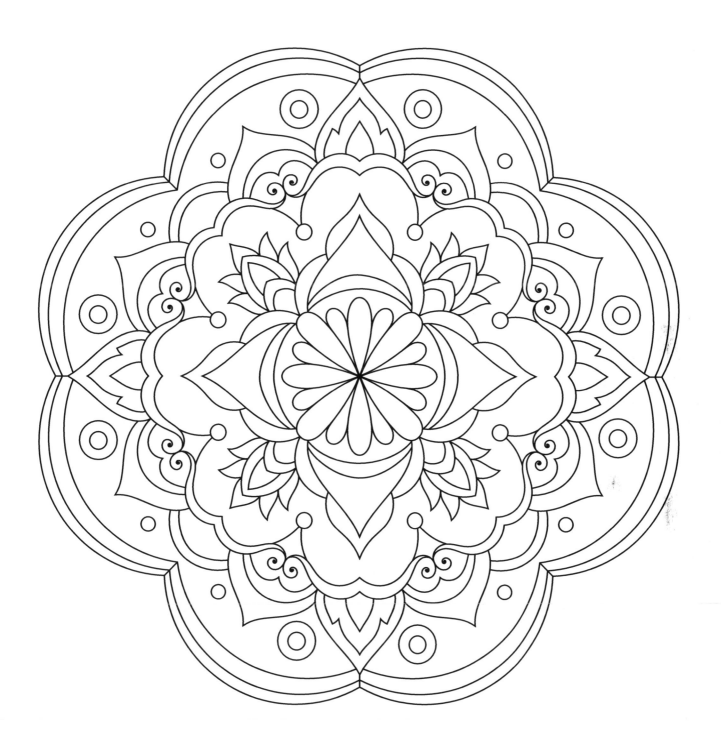

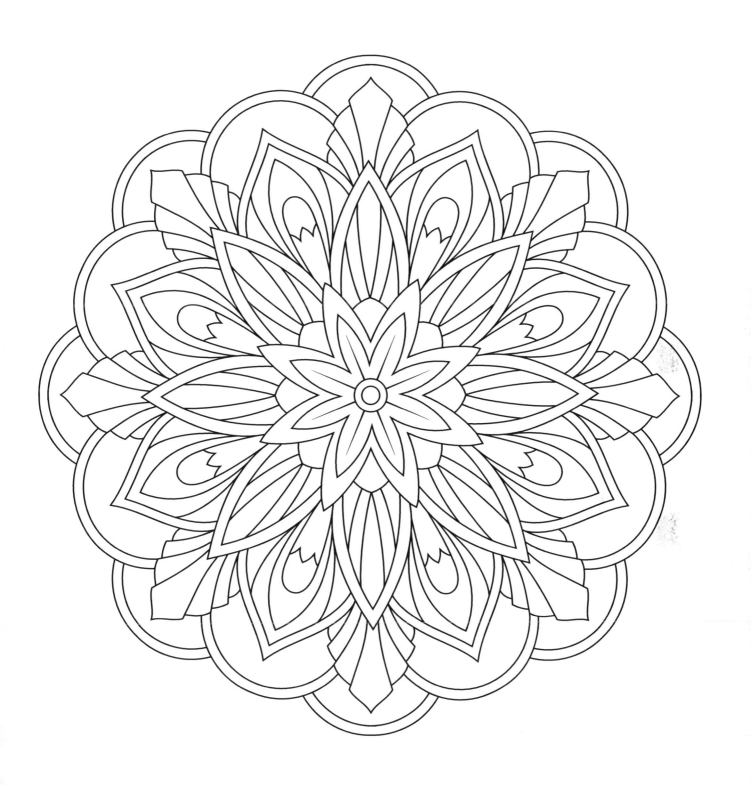

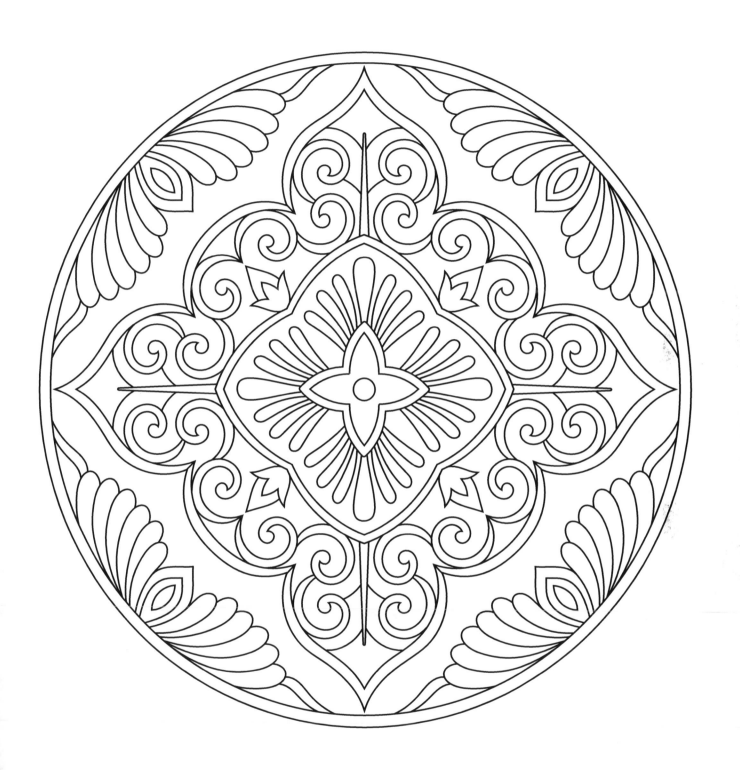

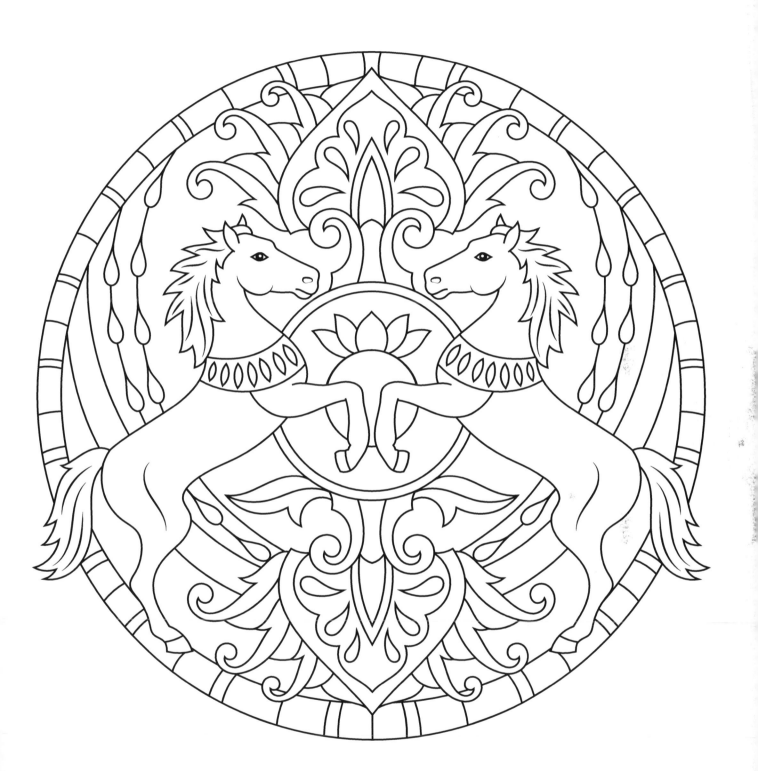

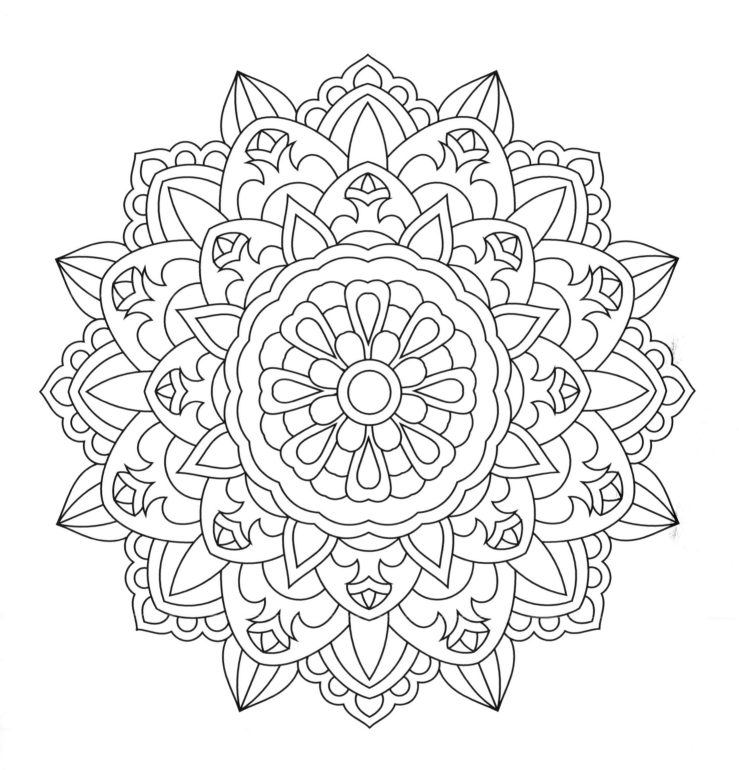

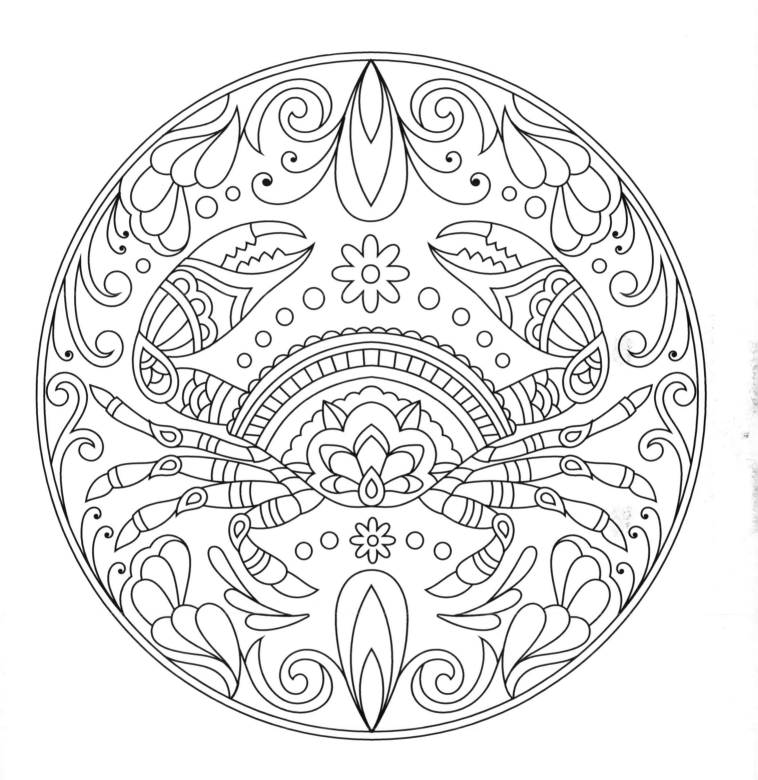

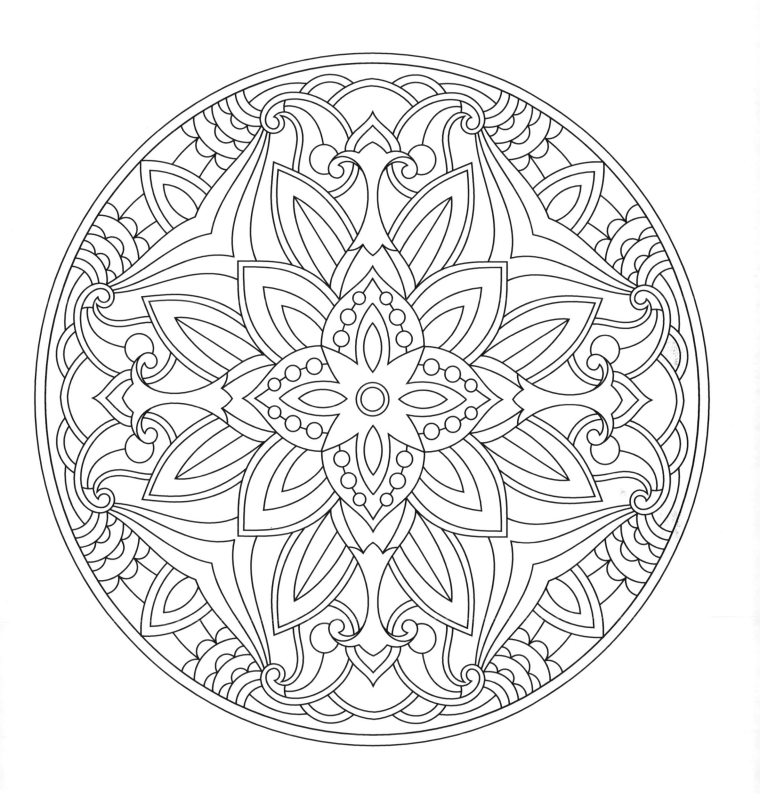

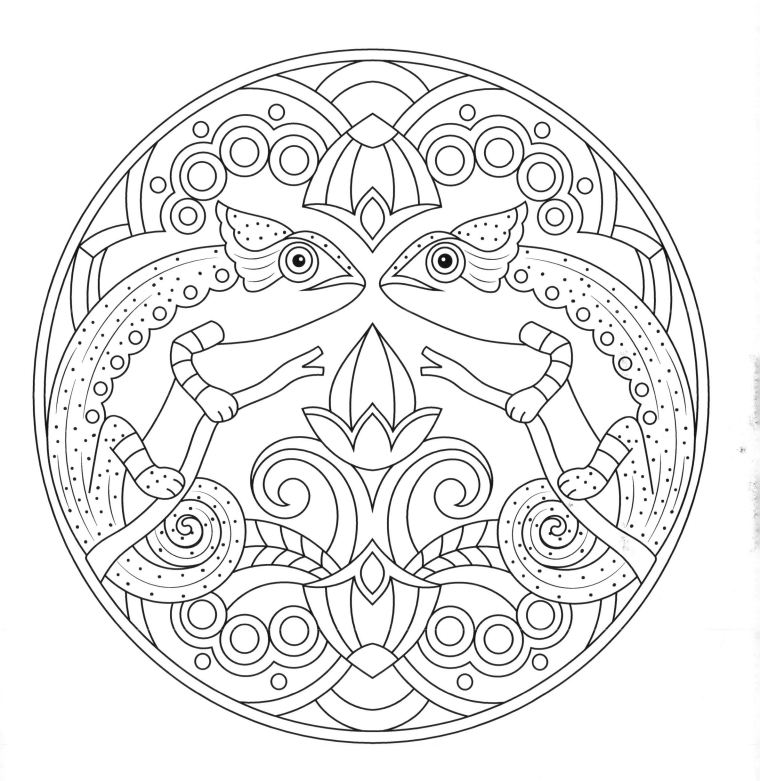

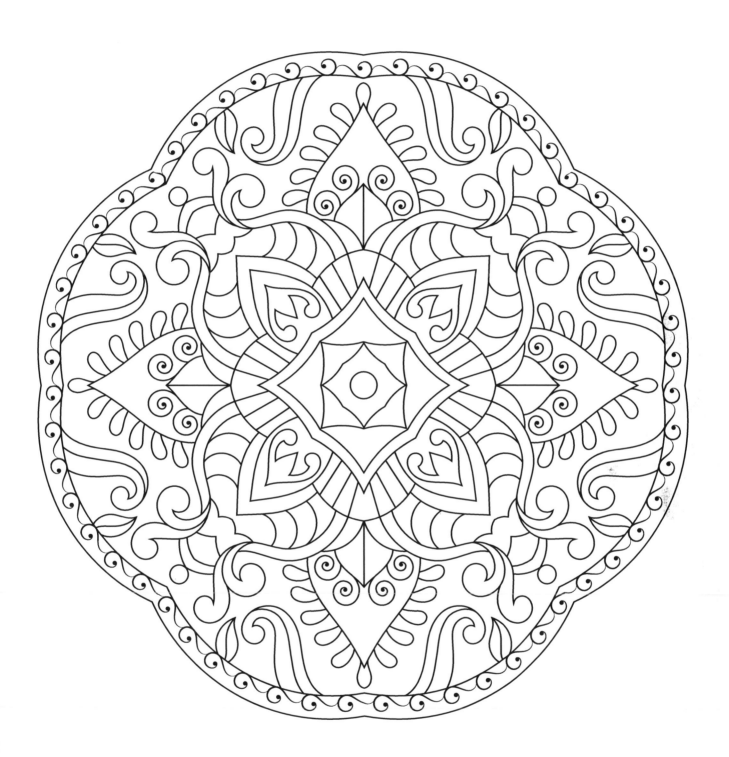

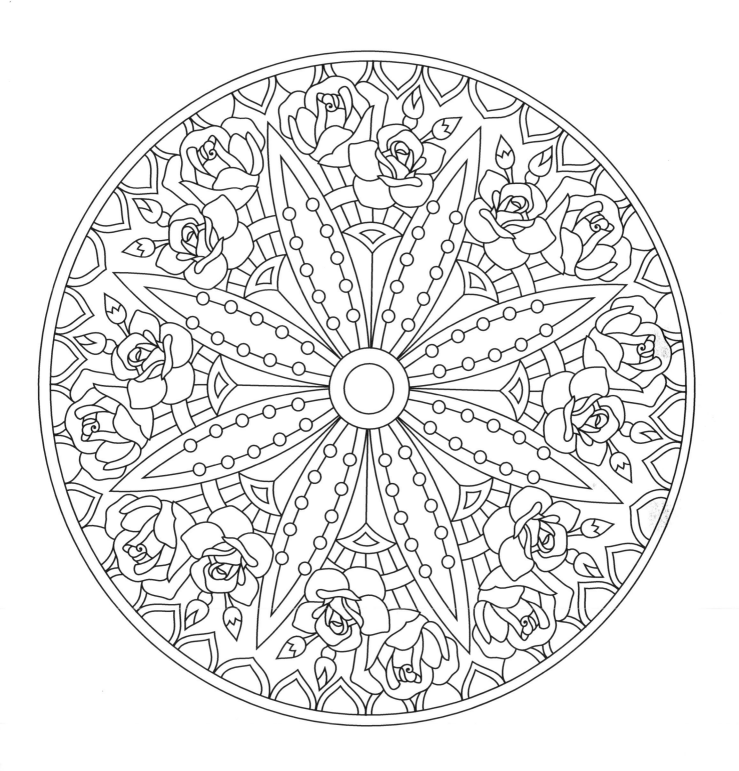

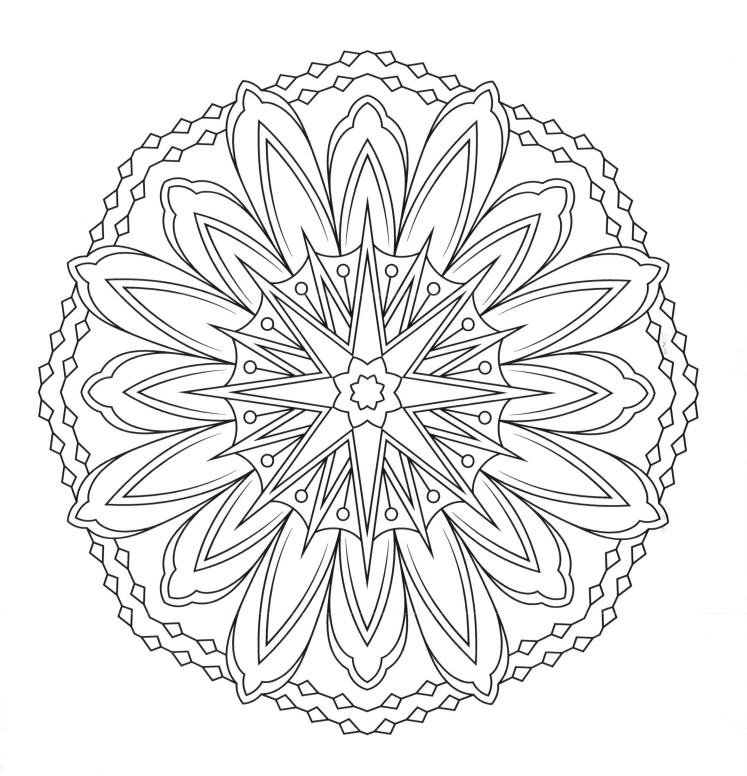

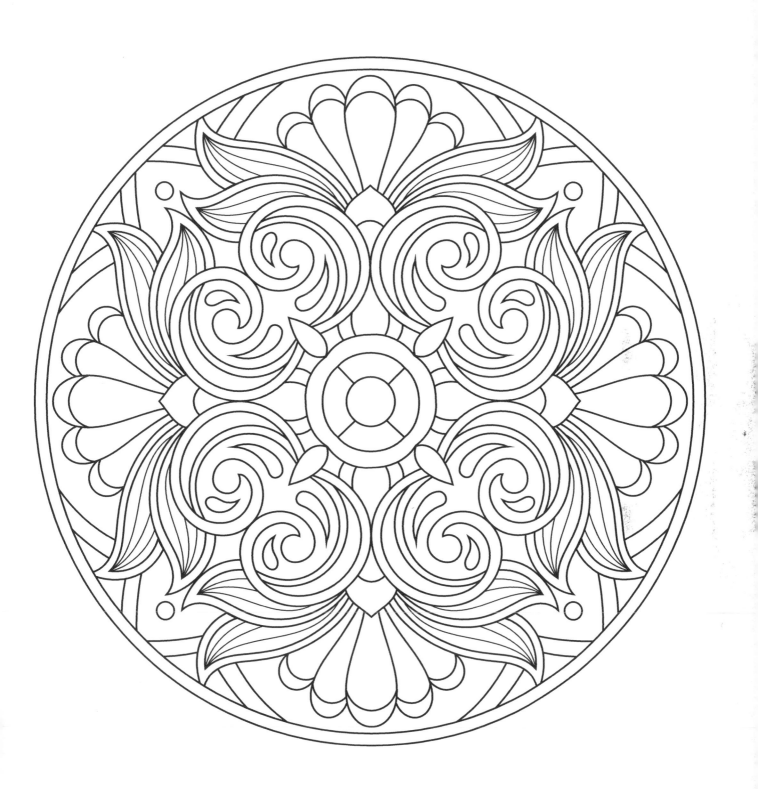

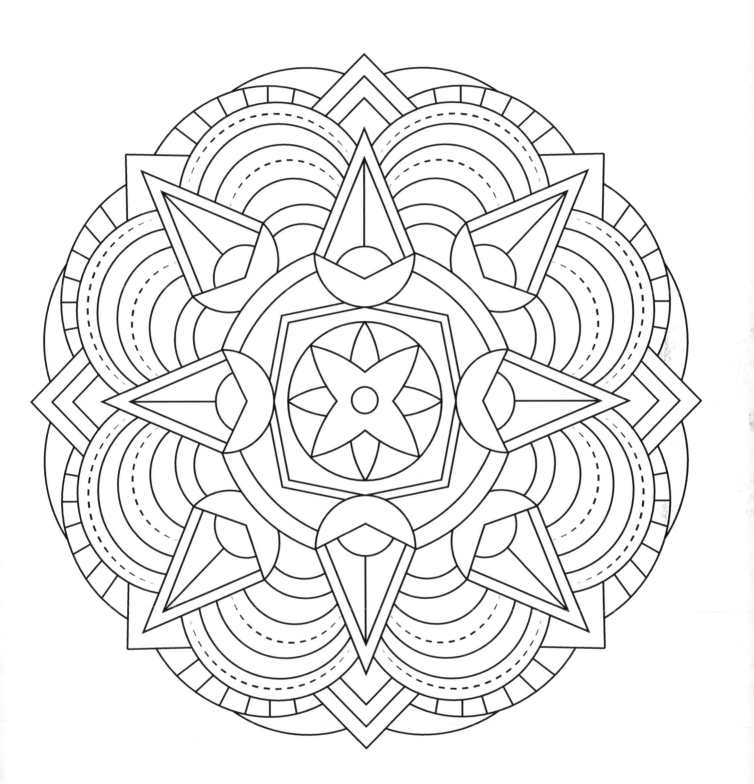

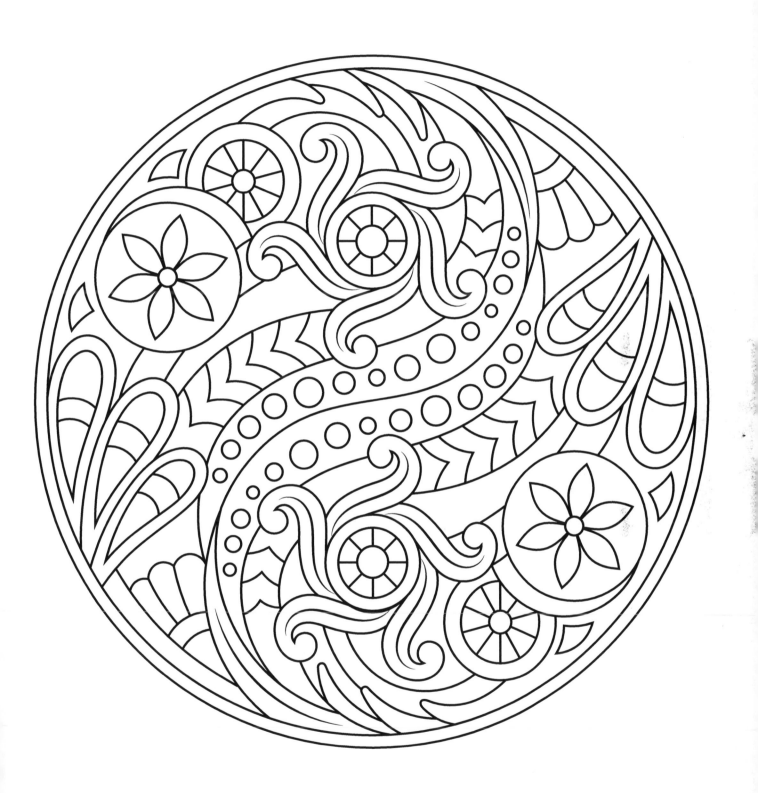

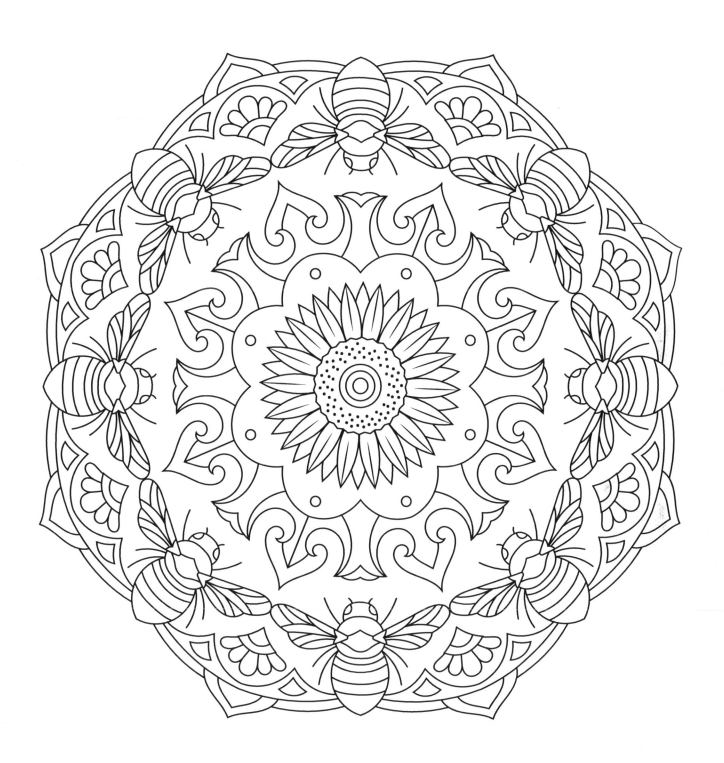

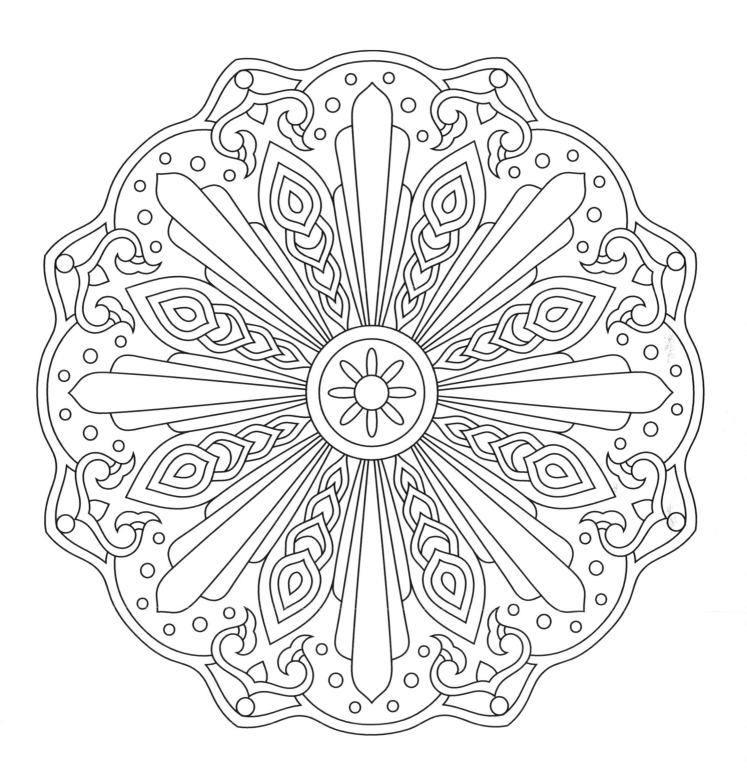

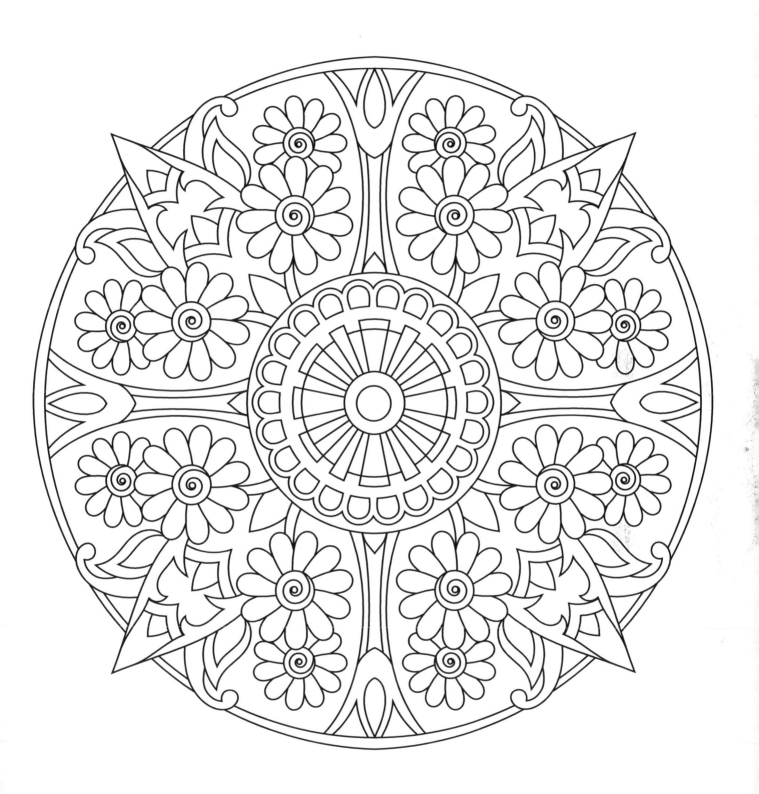

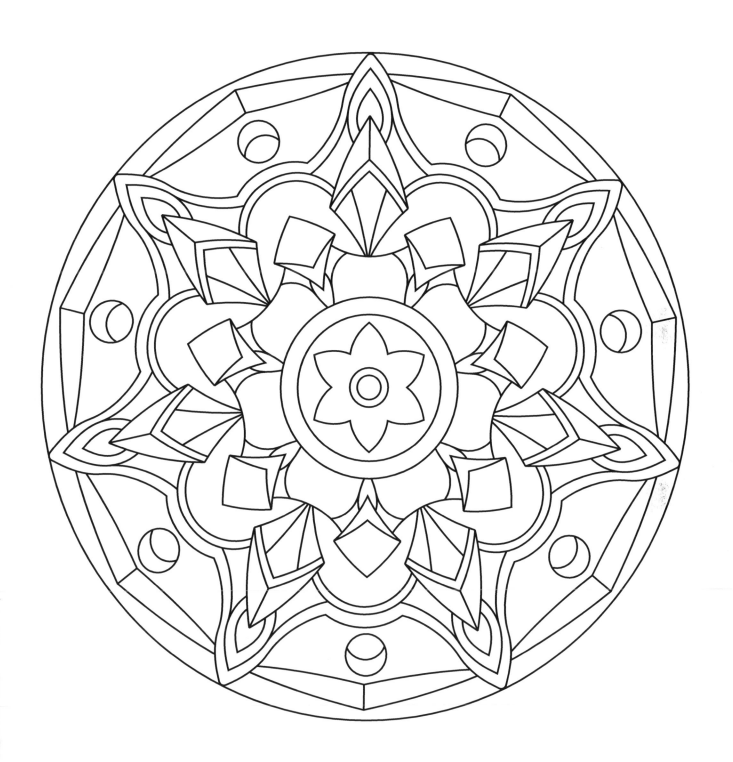

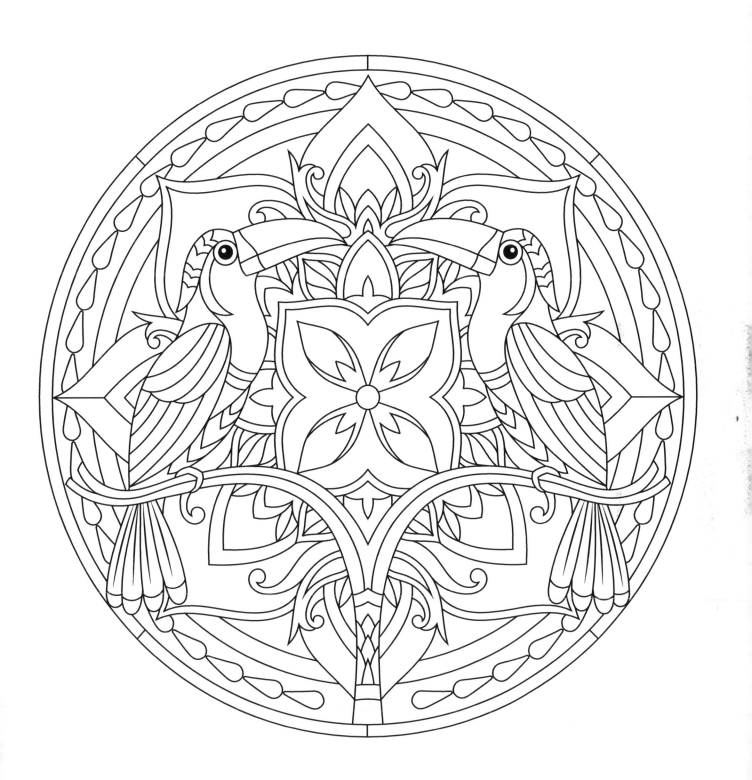

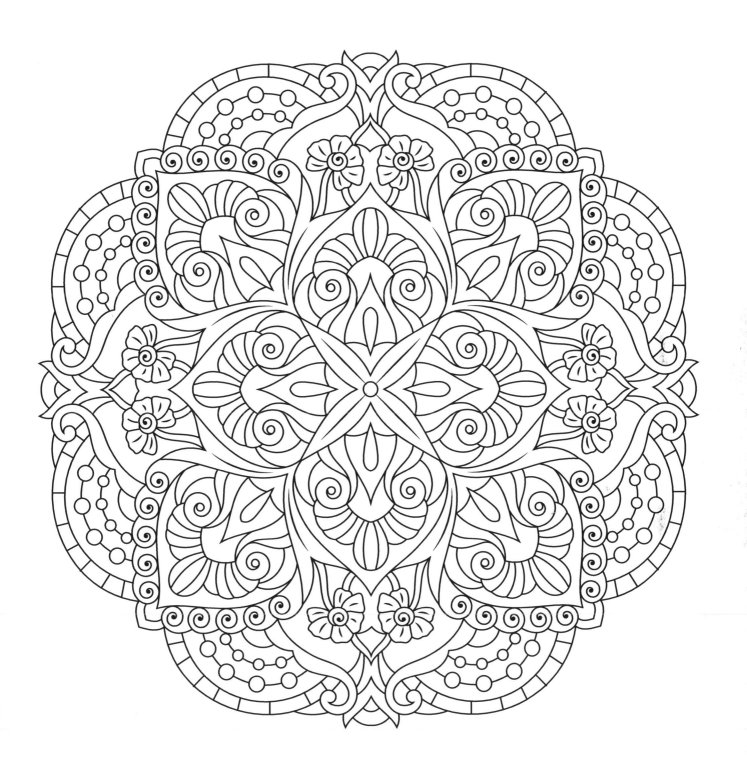

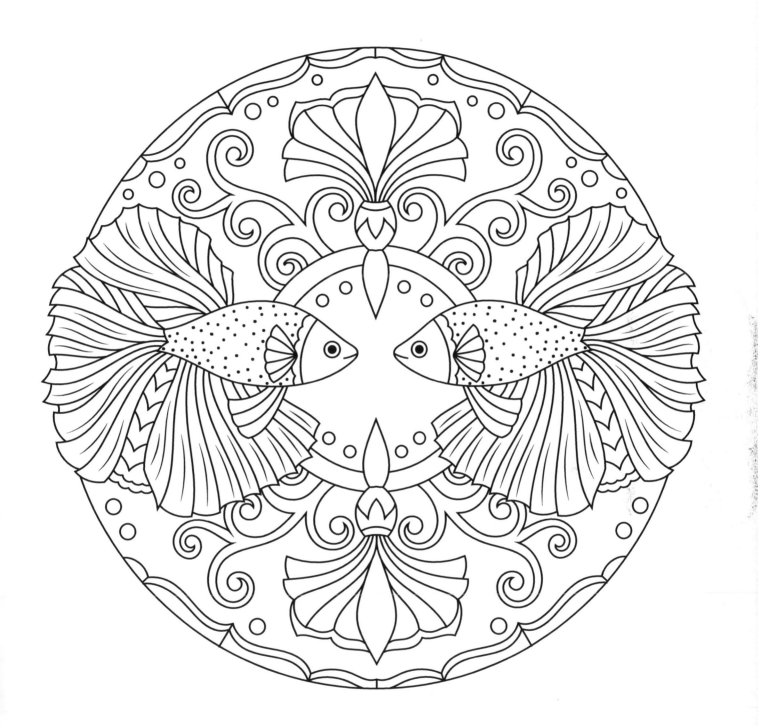

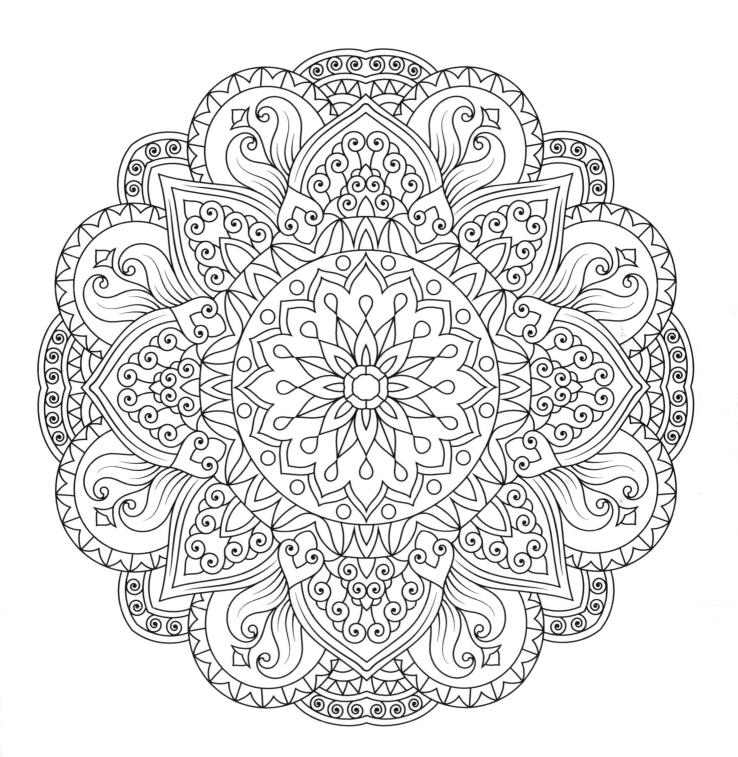

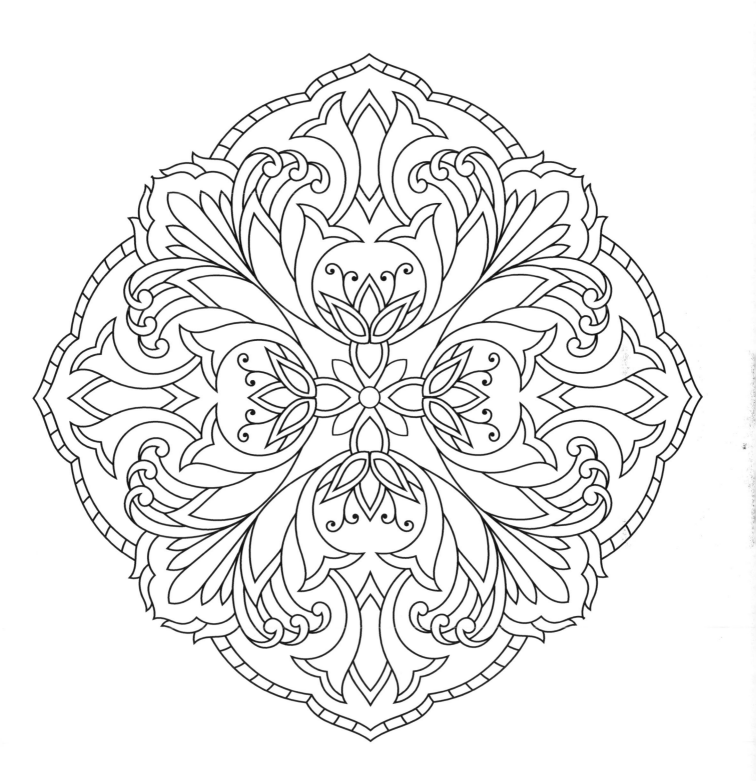

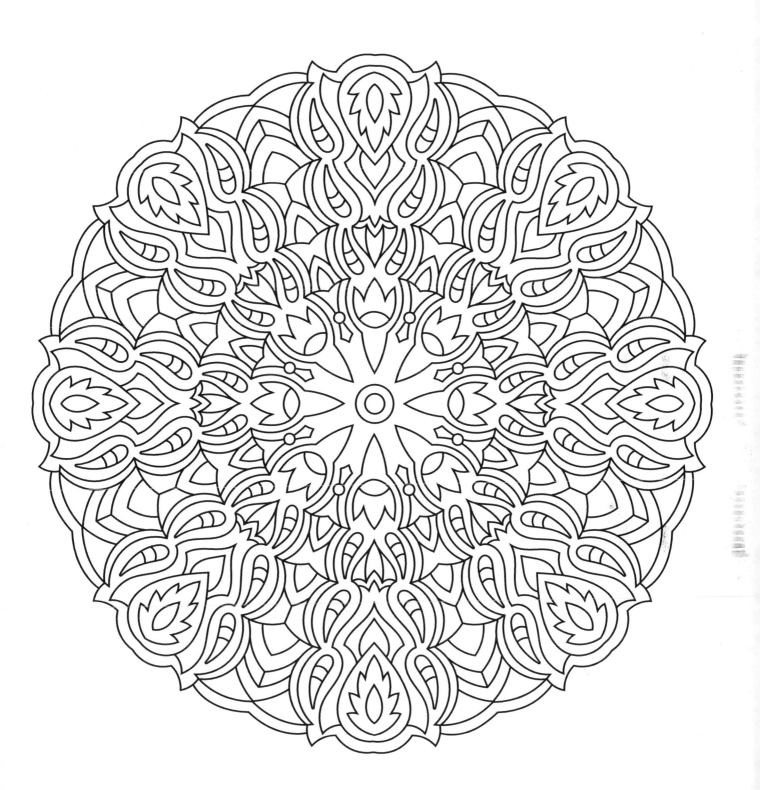

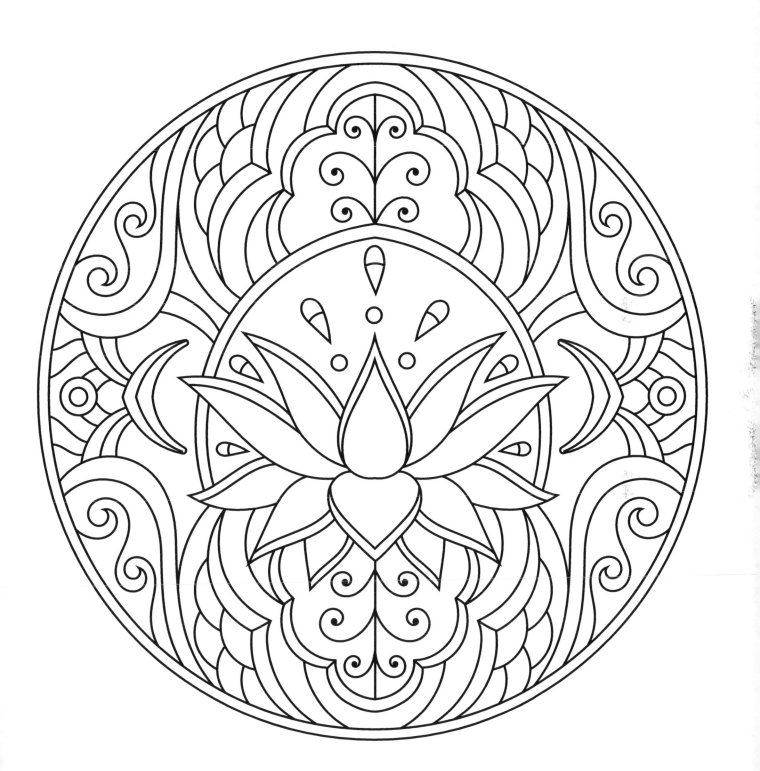

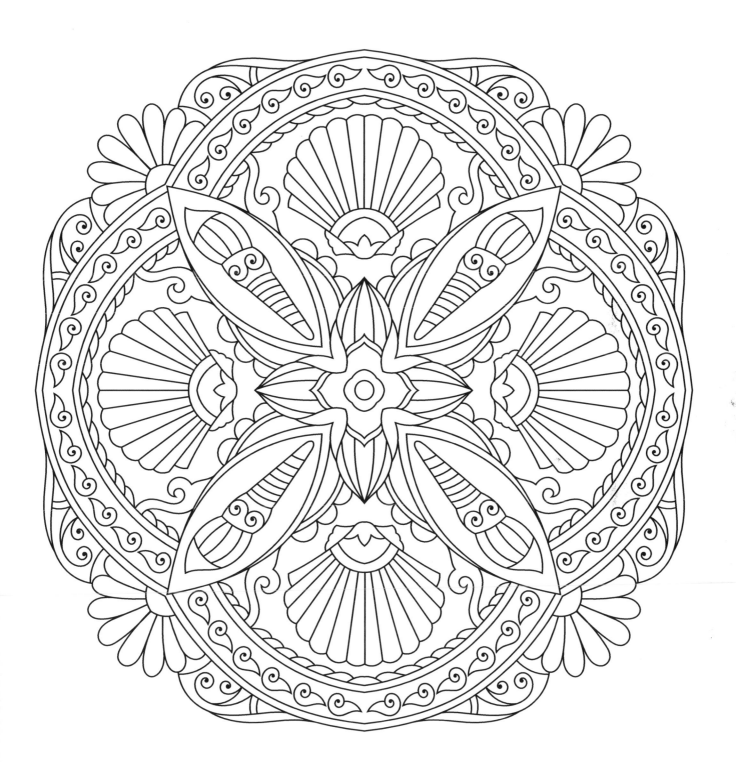

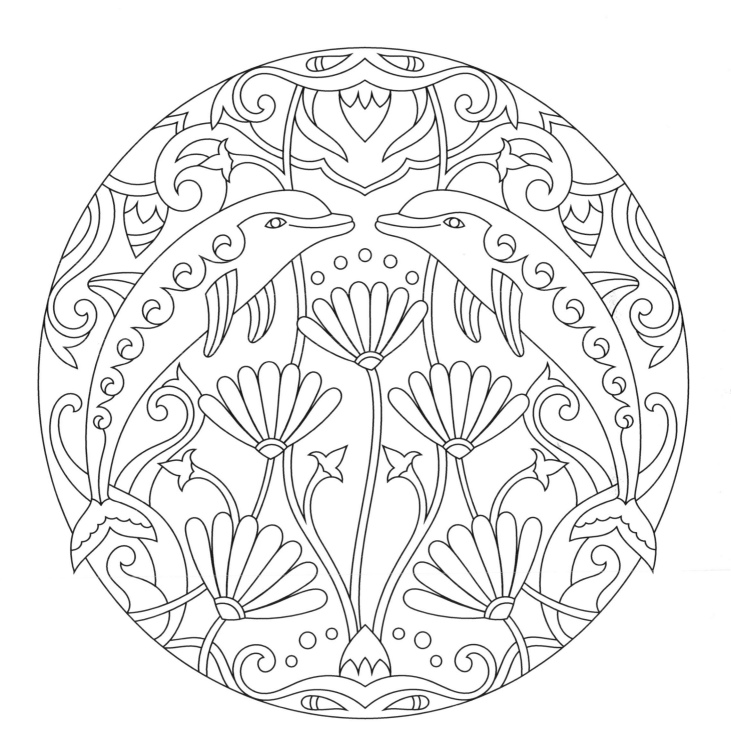

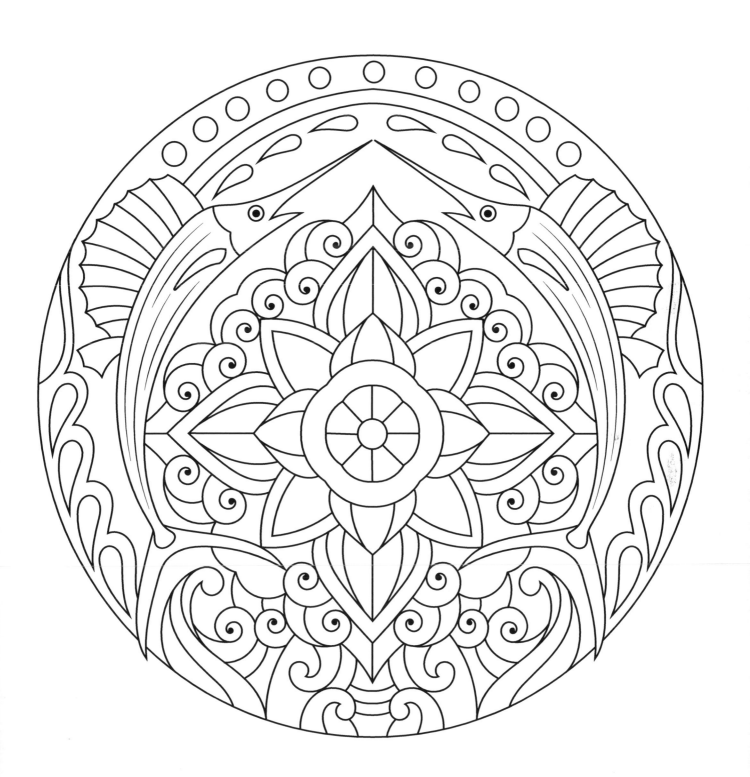

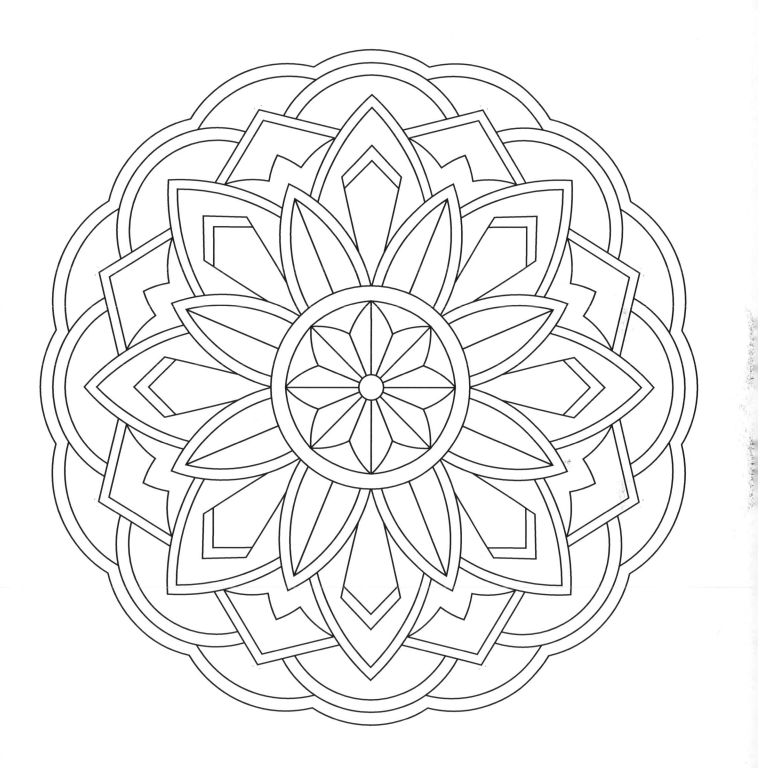

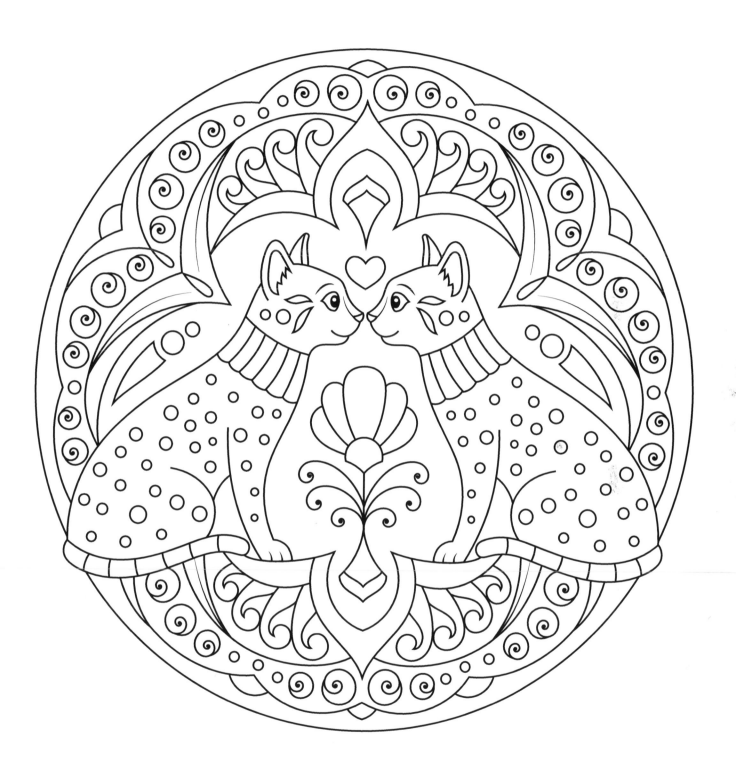

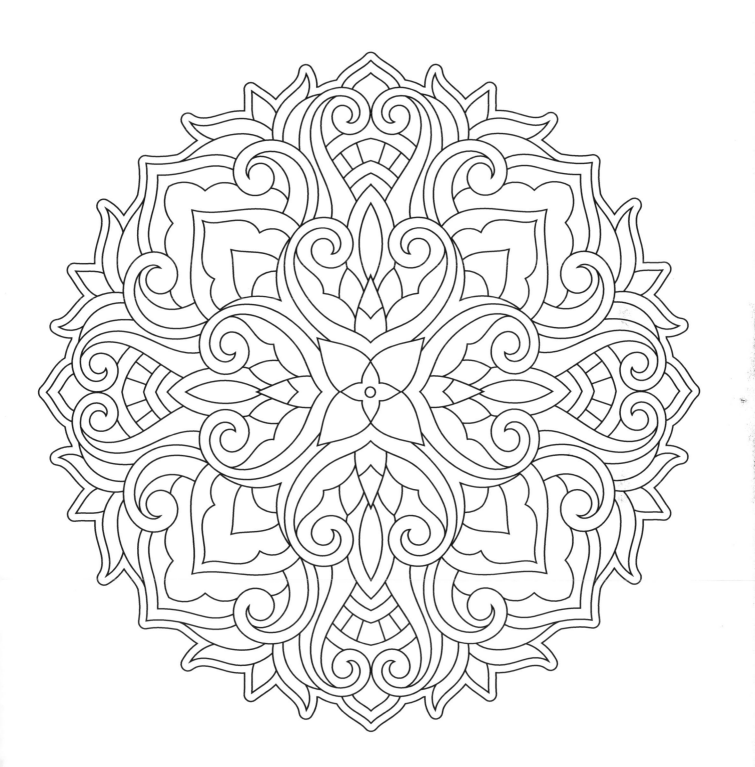

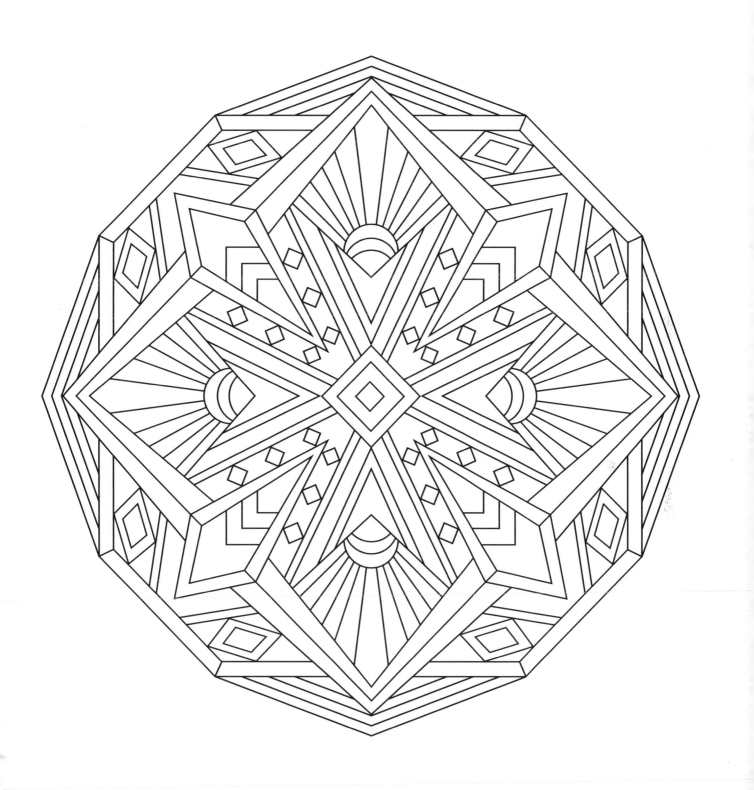

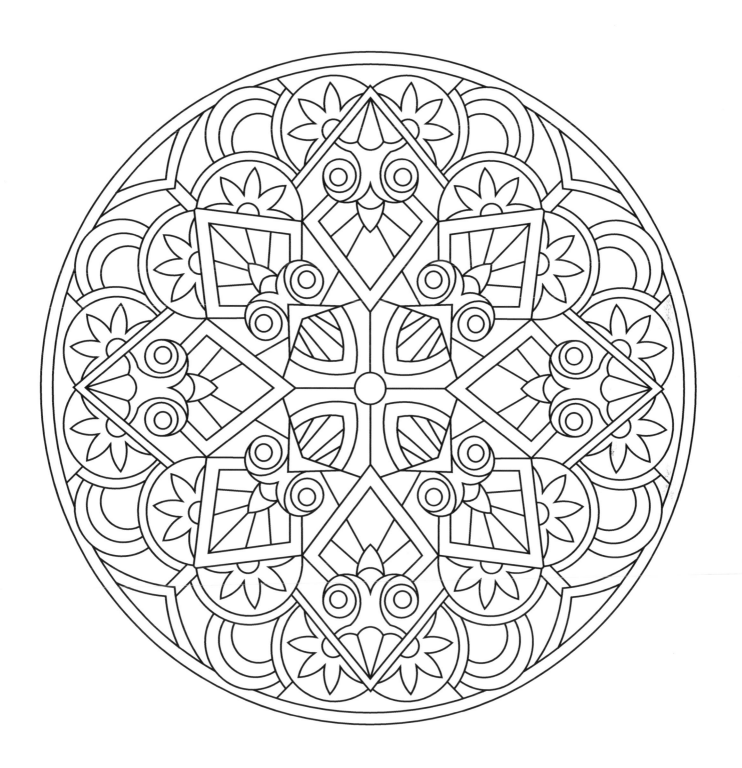

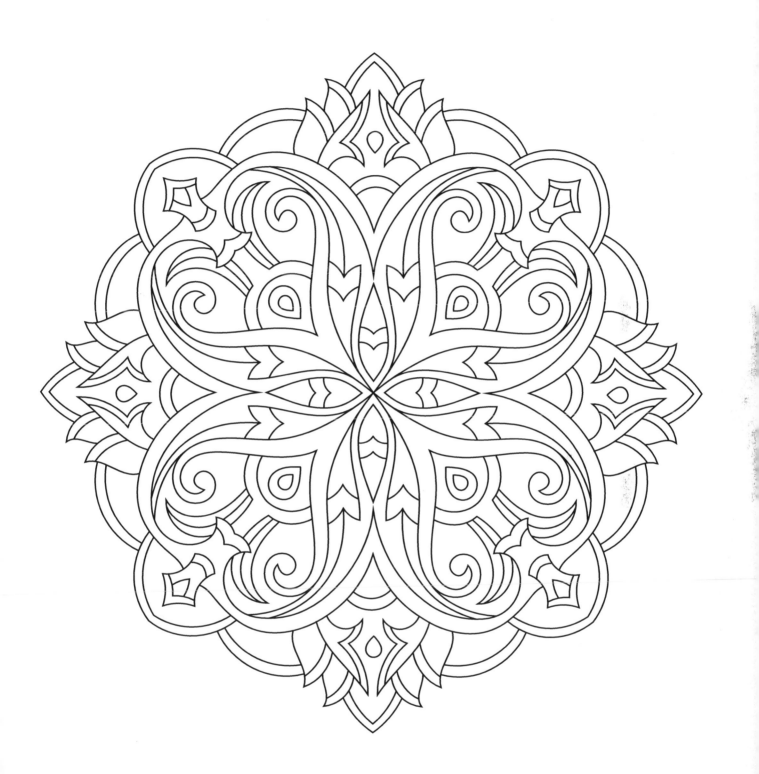

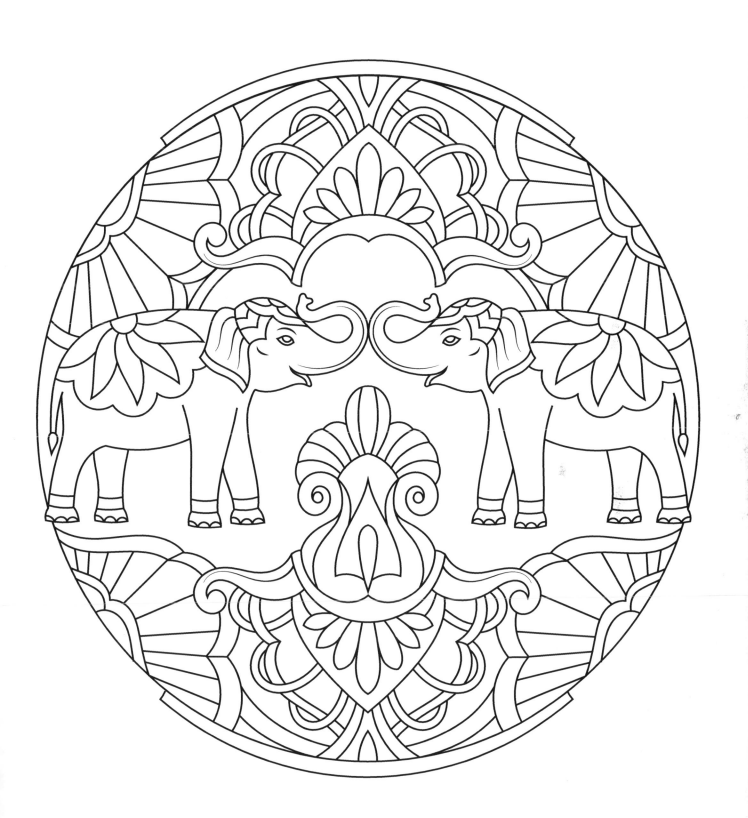

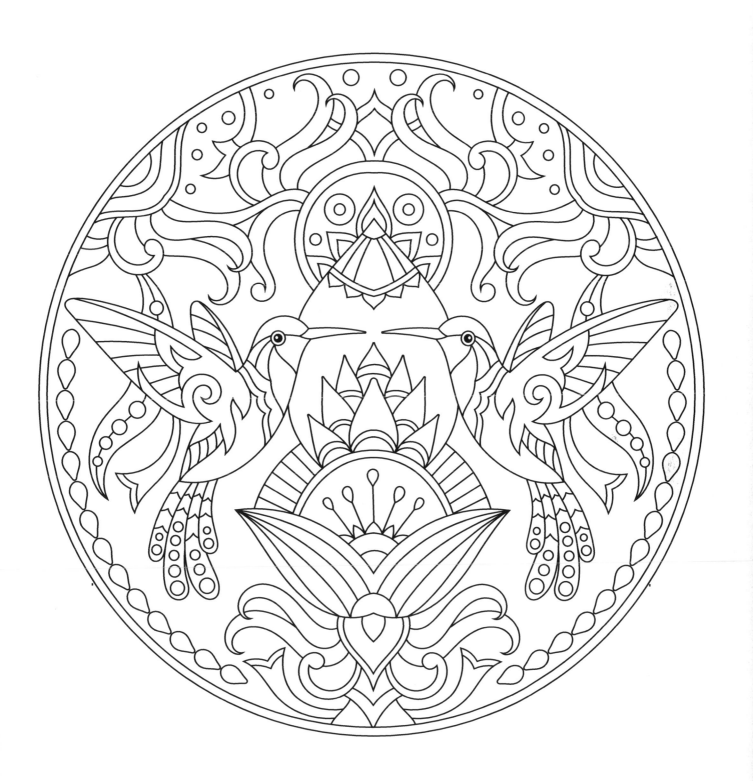

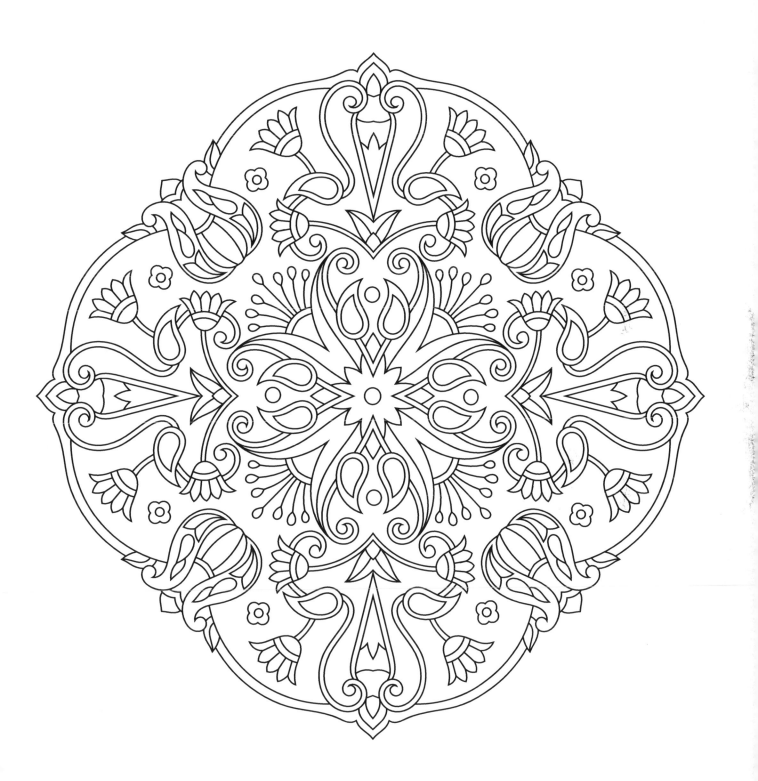

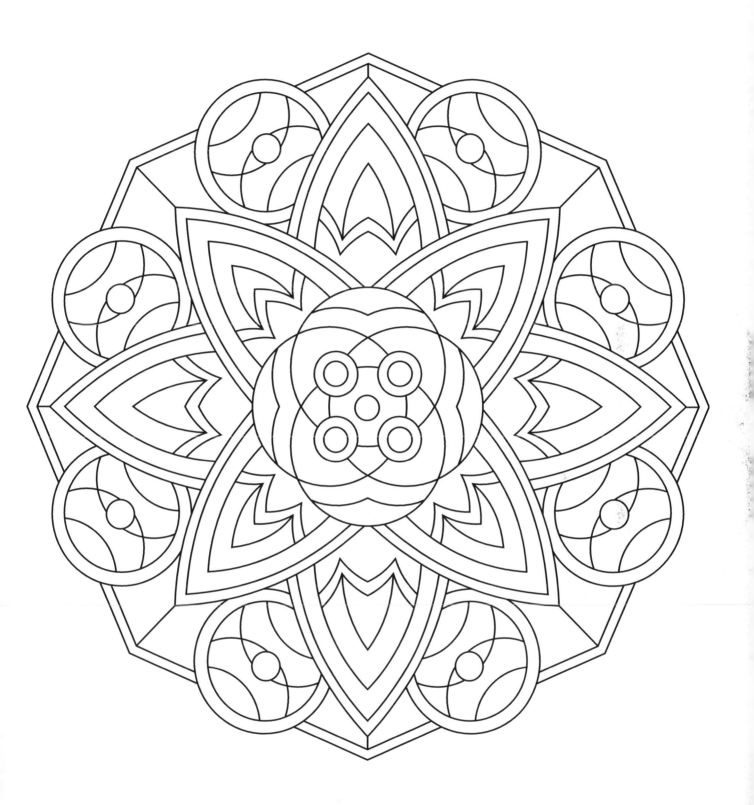

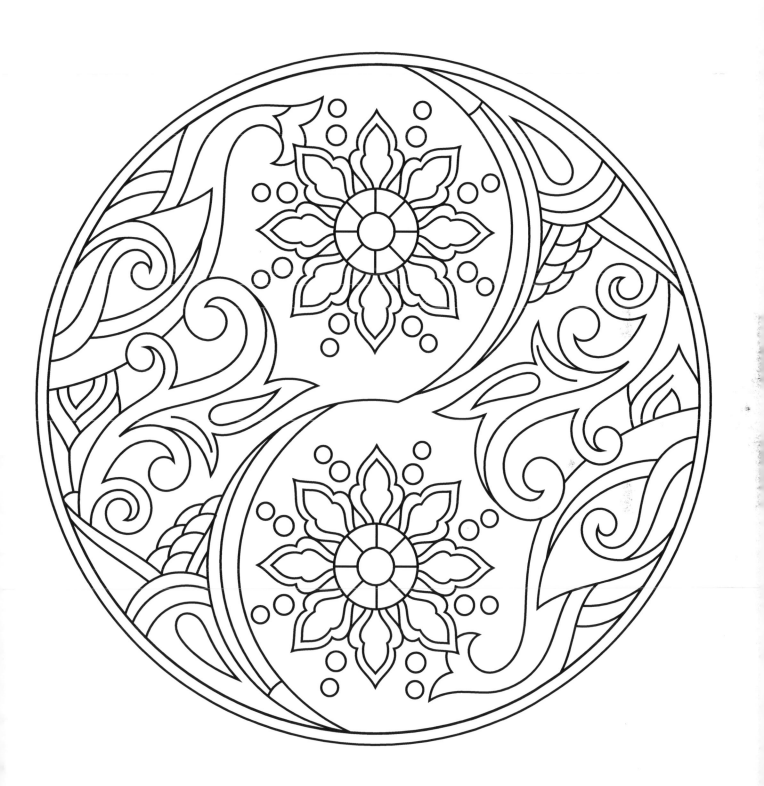

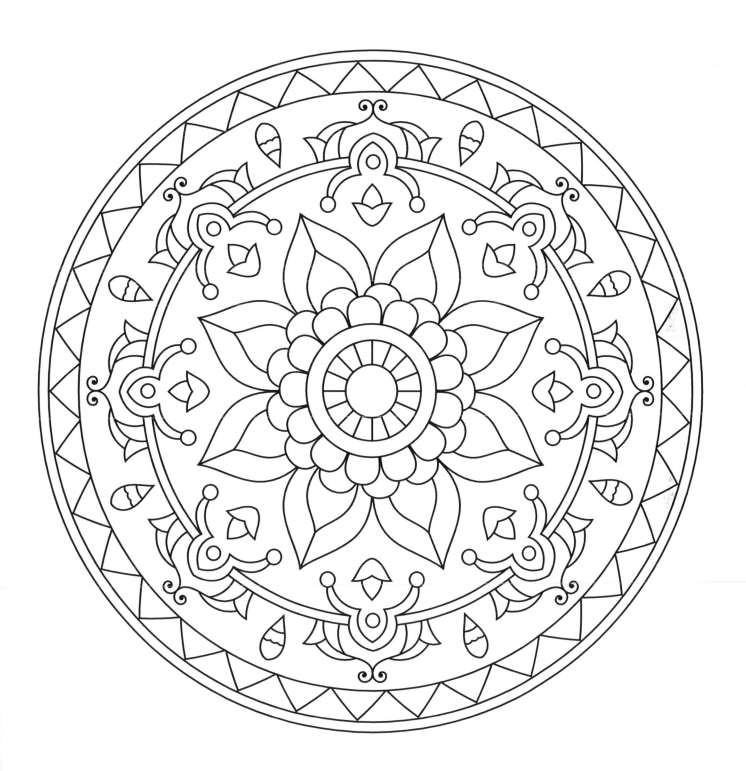

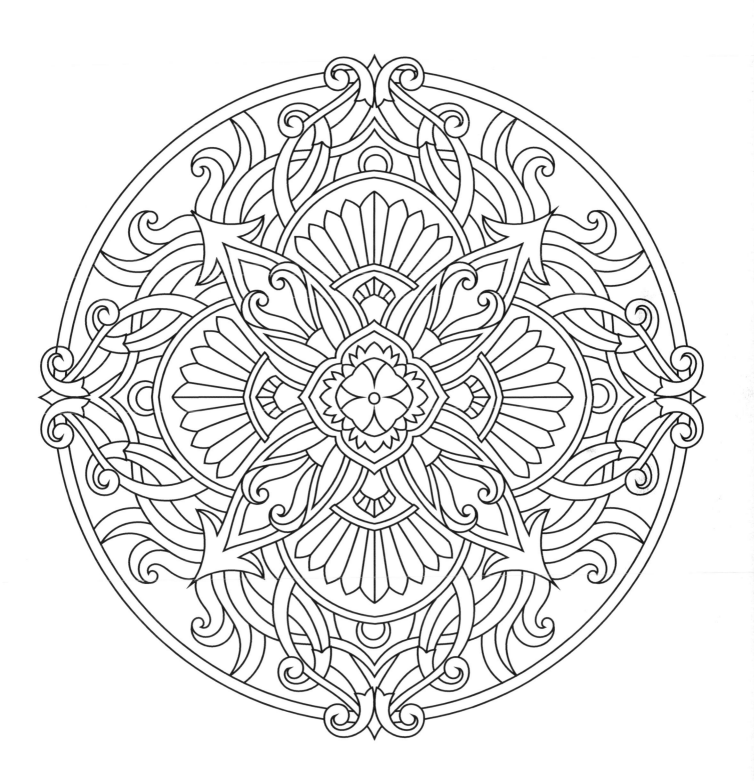

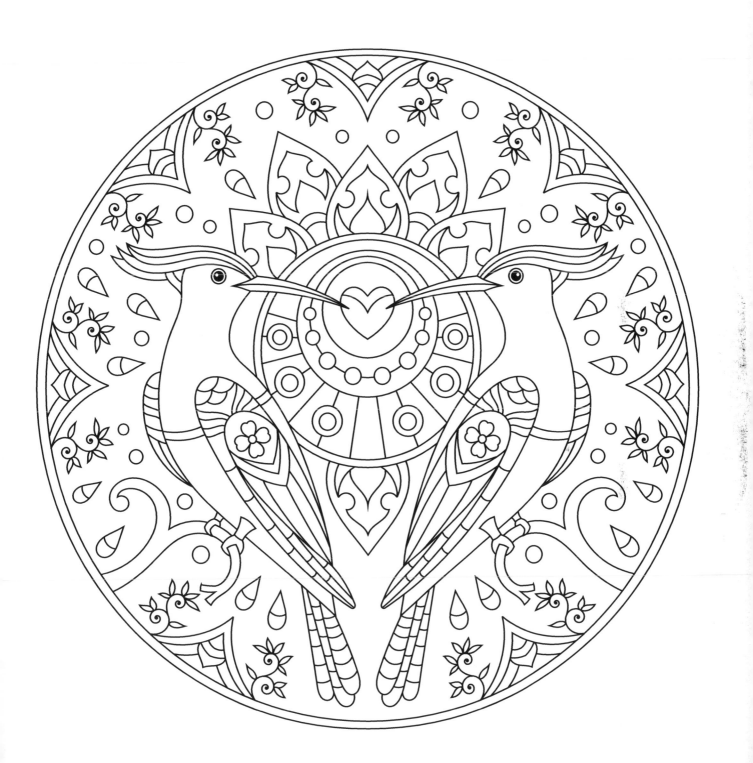

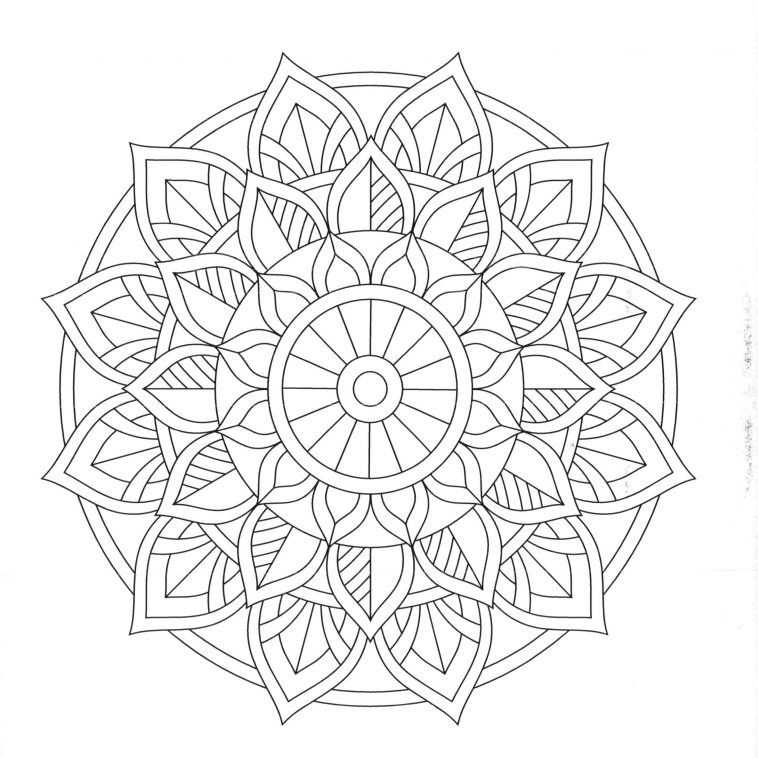

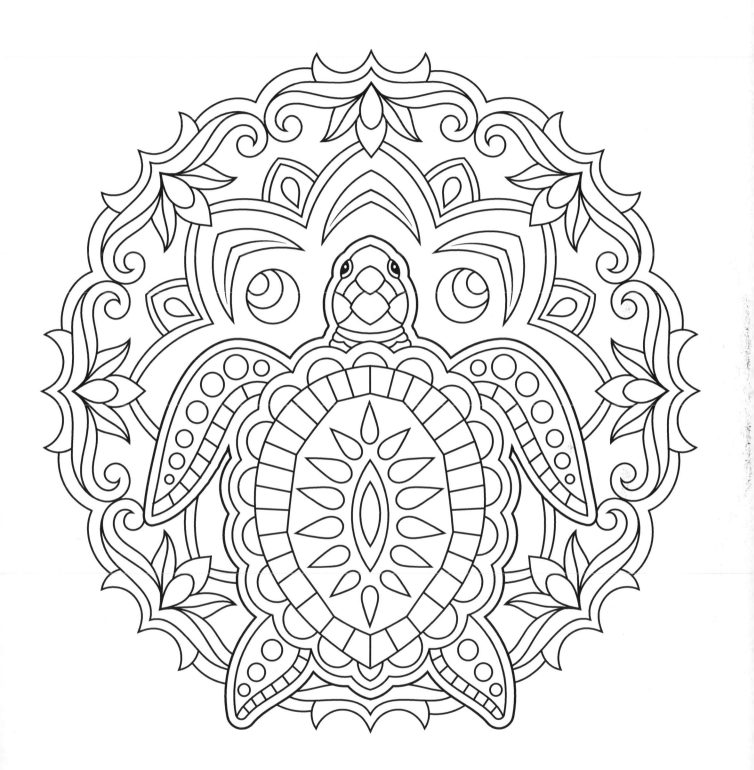

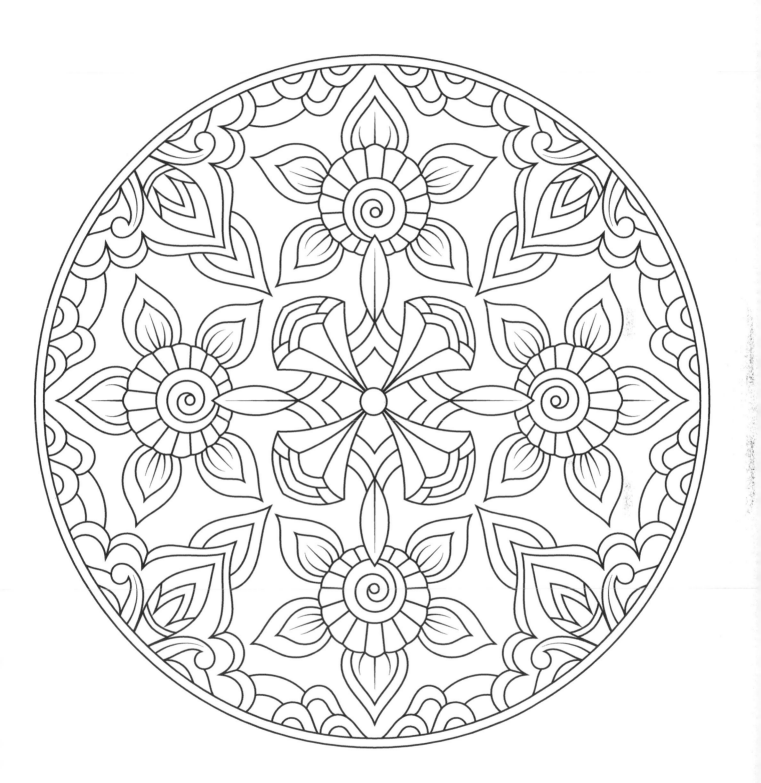

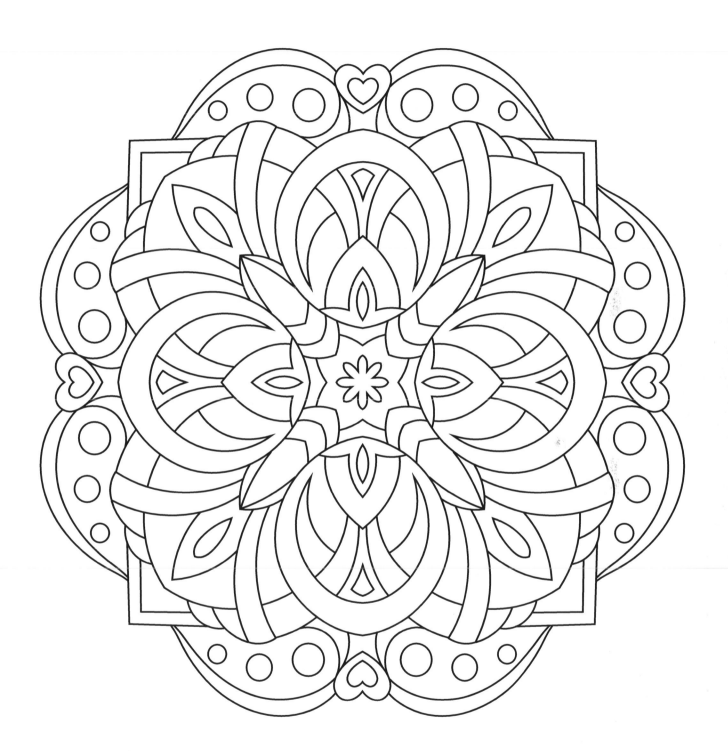

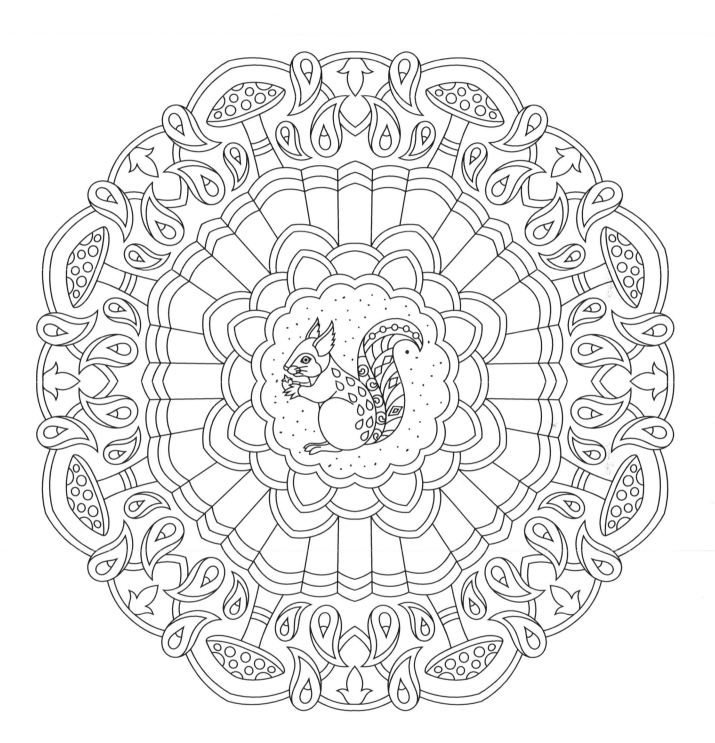

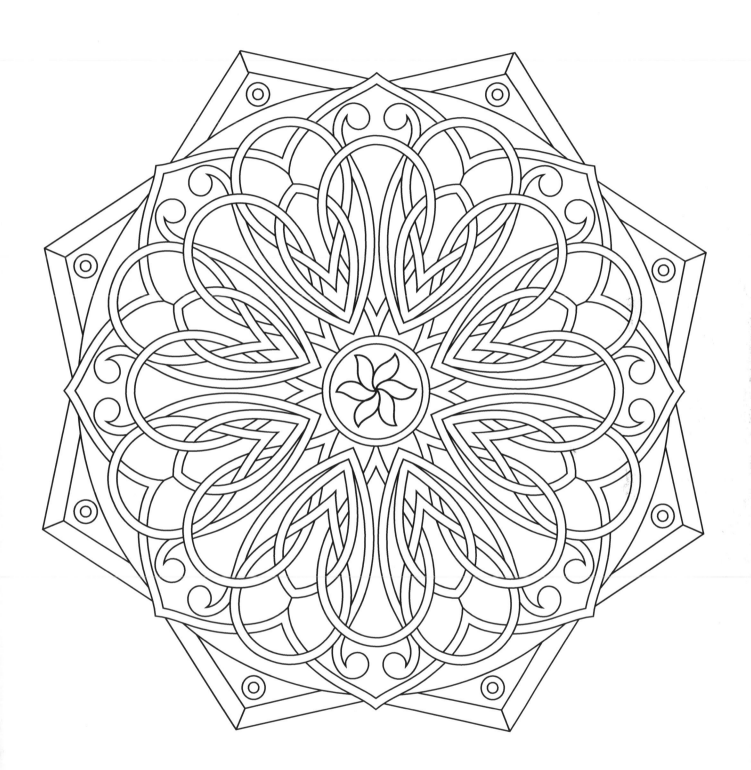

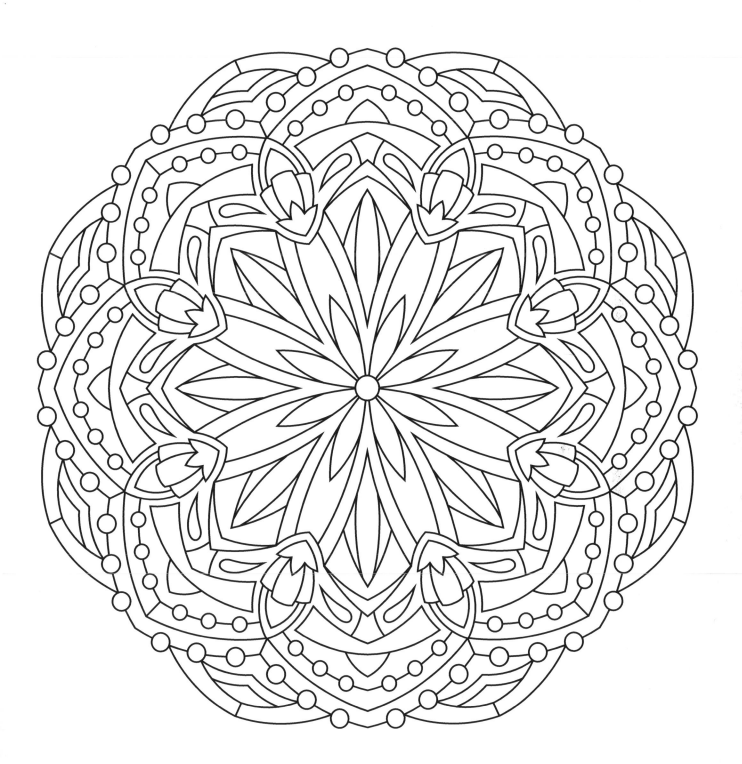

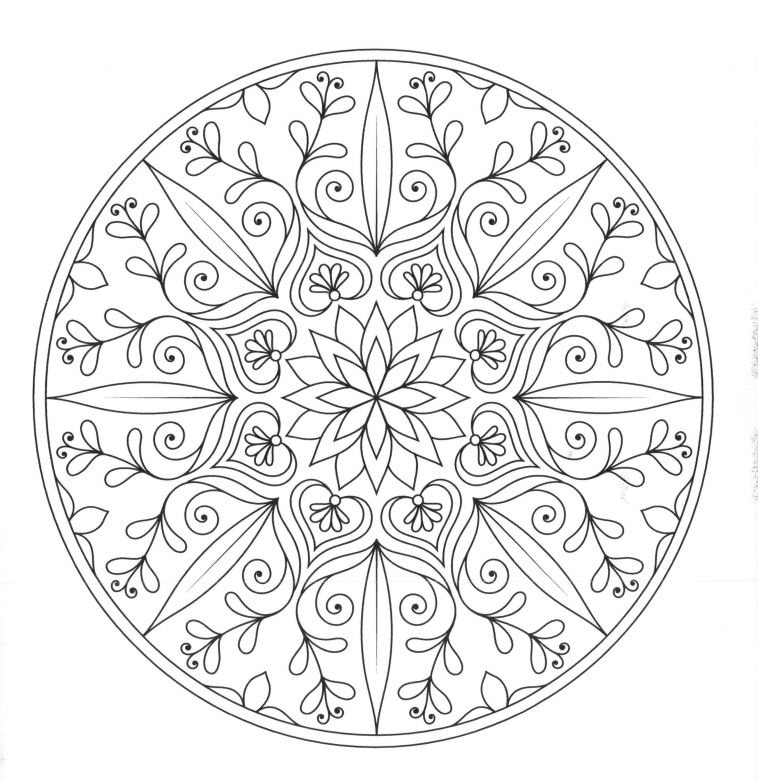

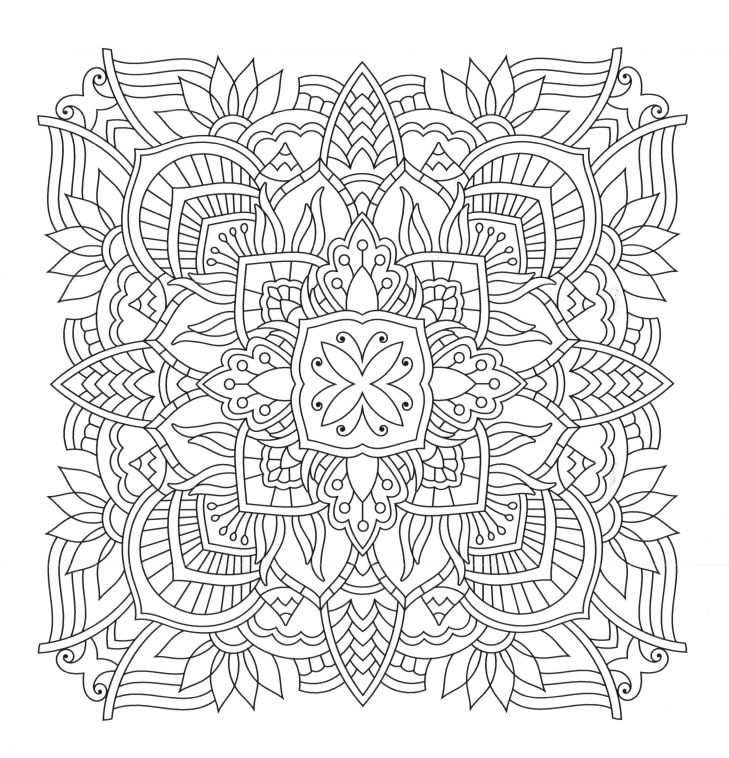

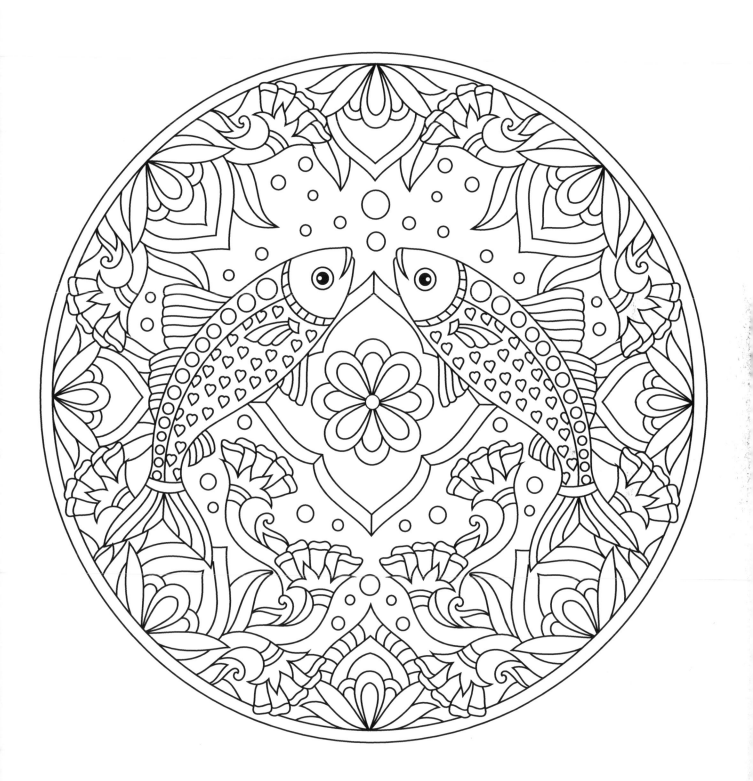

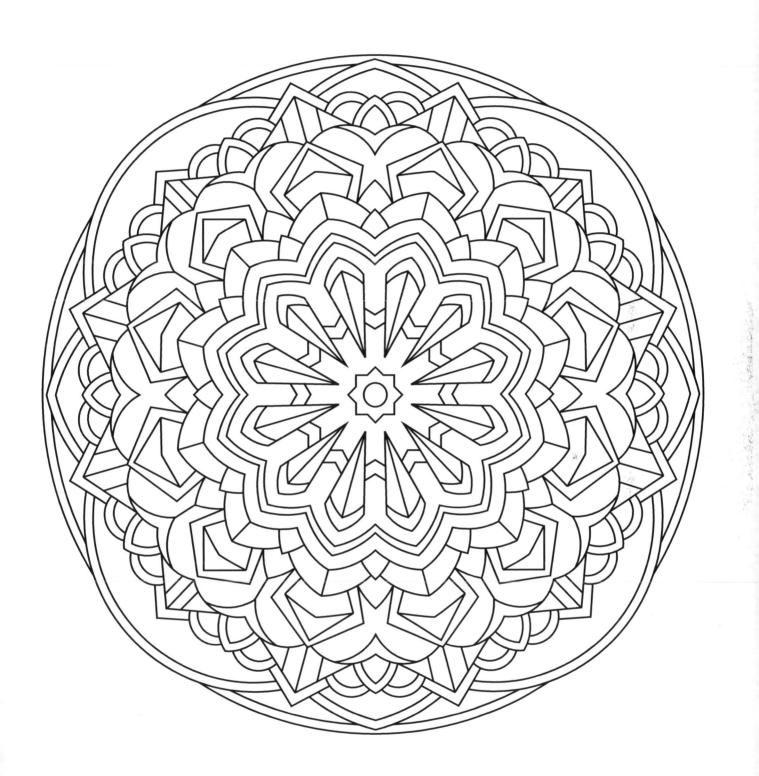

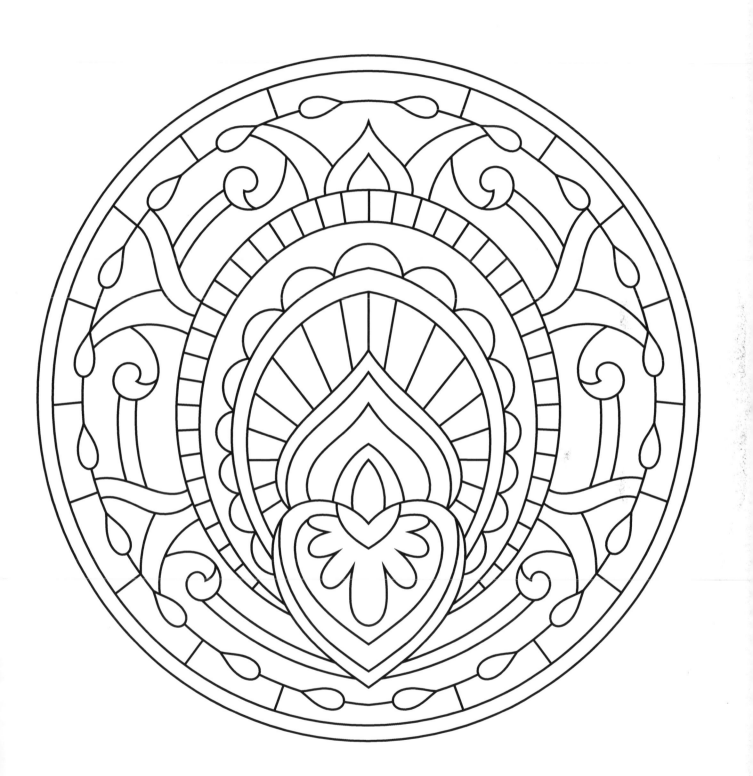

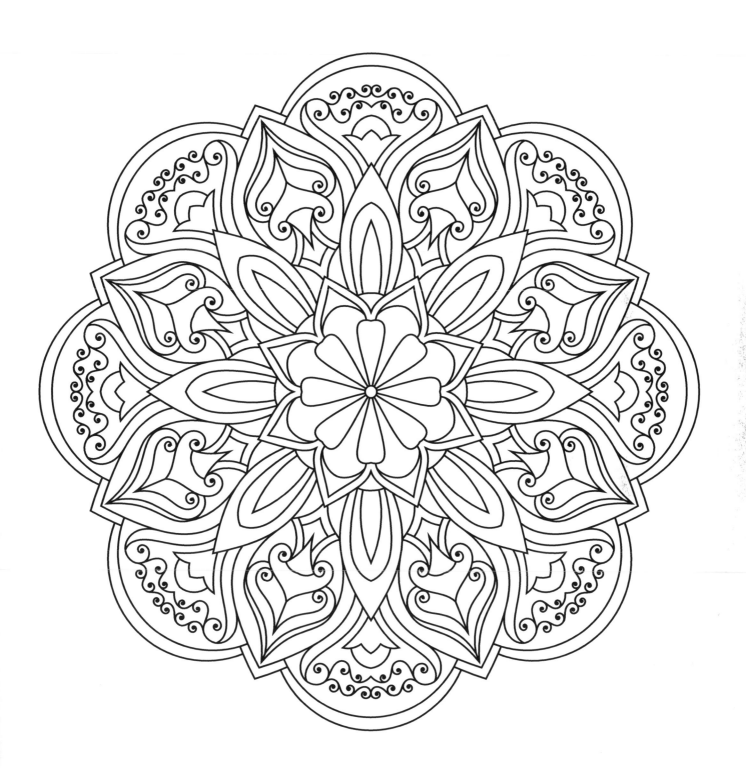

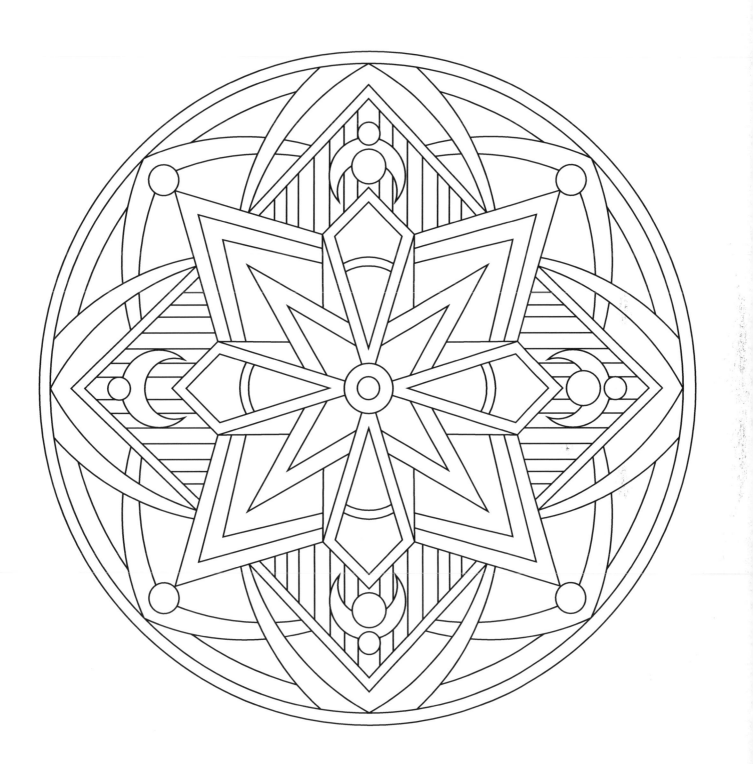

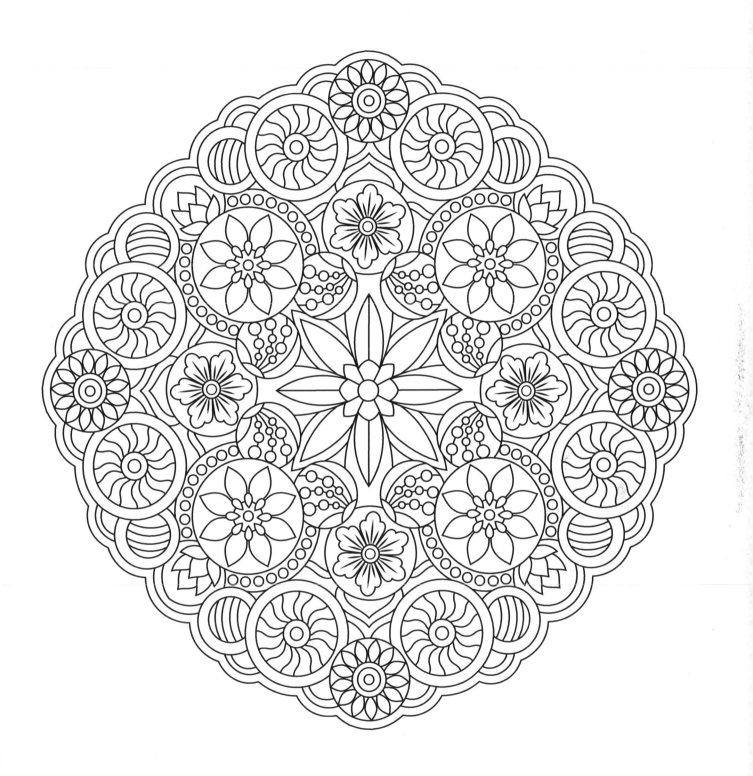

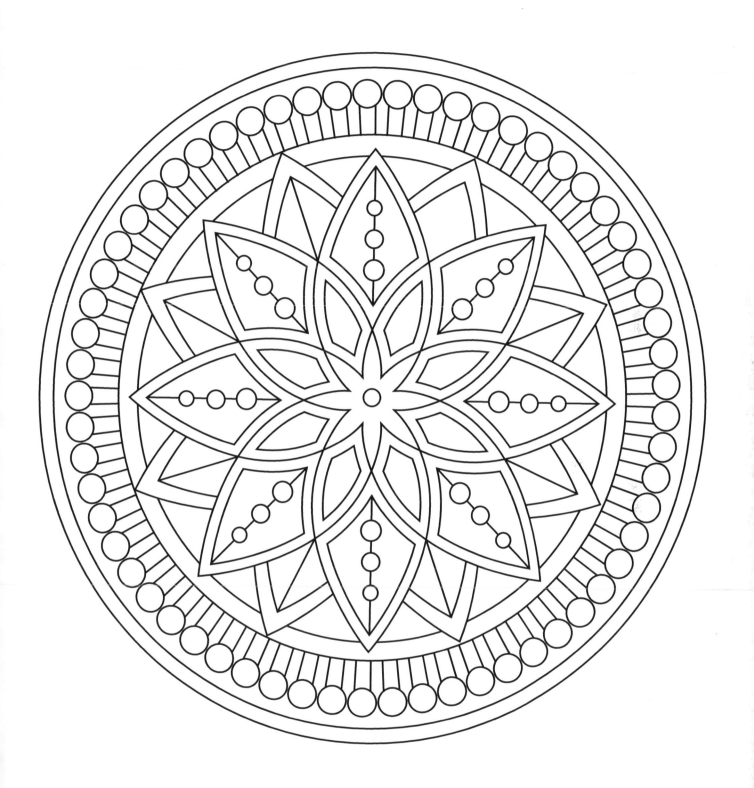

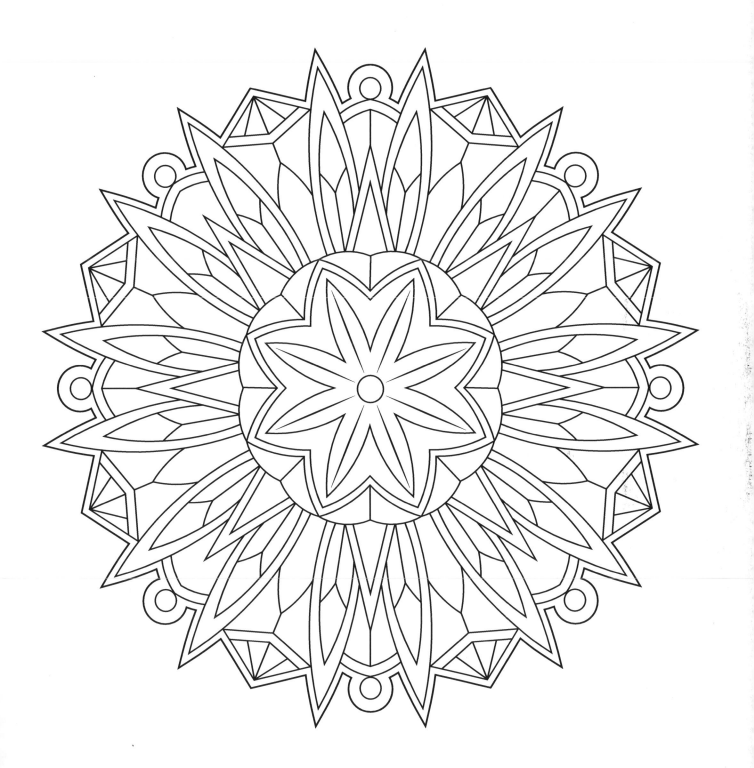

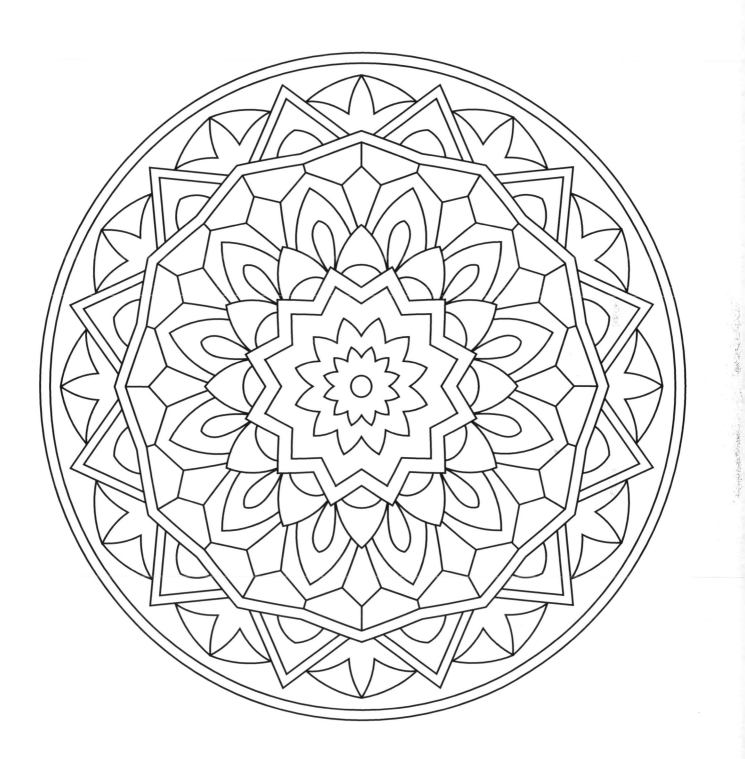

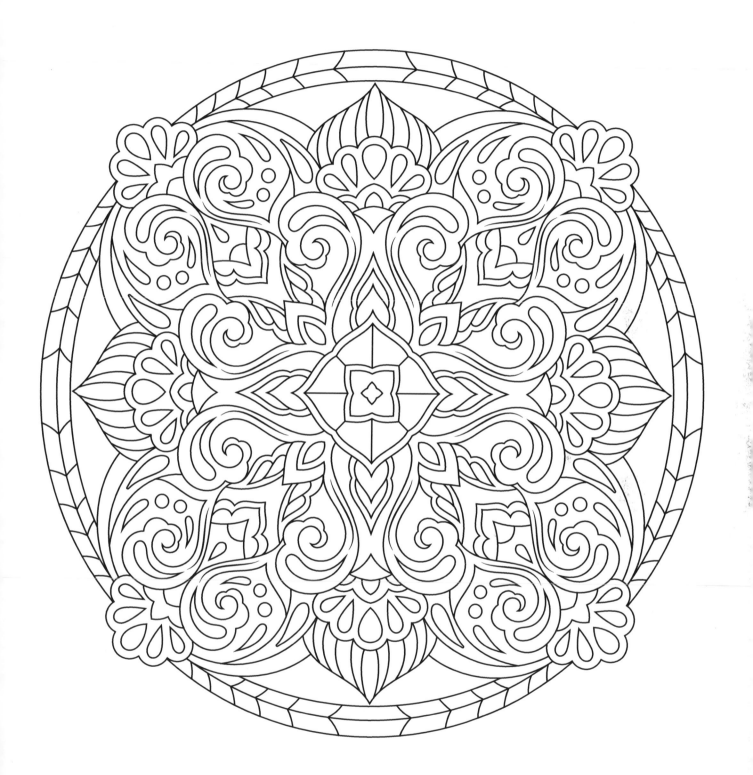

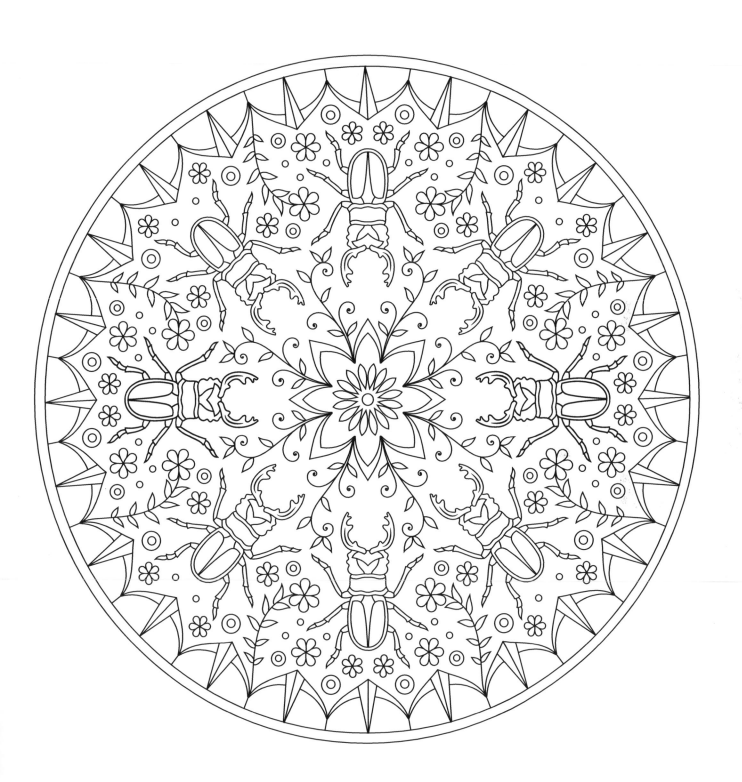

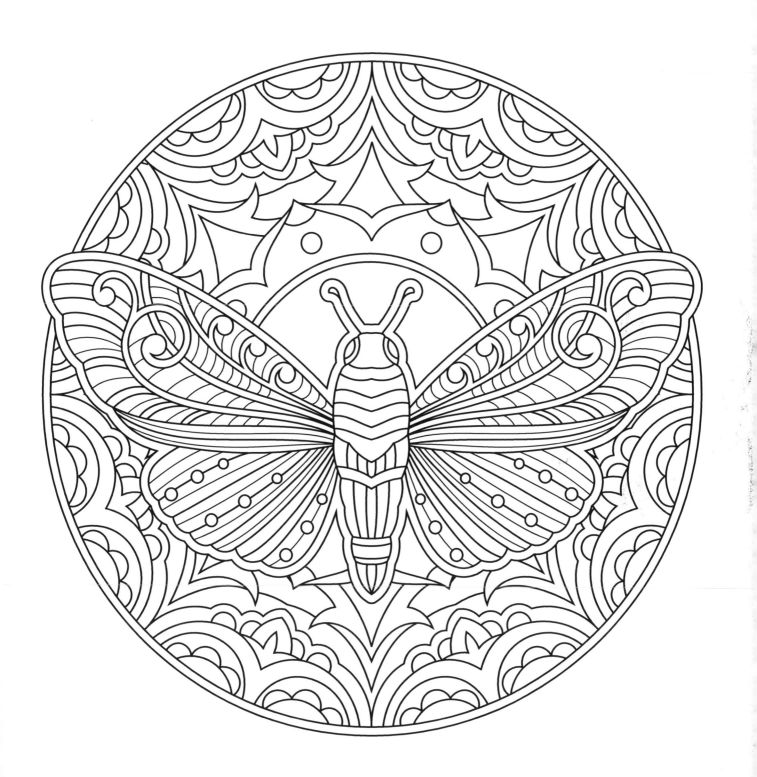

LEAVE MY AMAZON REVIEW

1. Go to Amazon
2. Search for *Jade Summer*
3. Find this book
4. Click the *Write a Review* button

JOIN US ON FACEBOOK

Facebook.com/JadeSummerColoring

Share your artwork, view artwork from other customers, and win free coloring books.

DOWNLOAD MY DIGITAL EDITION

Go to **JadeSummer.com** and provide us with:

Title: **Magical Mandalas**
Access Code: **72V89648**

Printed in Great Britain
by Amazon